Praise for *I Only V*
by Doyle Hollister

"A dream loves to be met in the way of a dream. Doyle Hollister meets his beloved, Nature's dream, in this deeply personal, genuinely intimate account of the wilderness surrounding his childhood home. His words offer an experiential account of what for most goes unseen, the majesty and mystery of the natural landscape. At Hollister Ranch, Doyle guides us through a breathtaking story of surviving a fast-moving almost "supernatural" lightning-and-thunder storm. With an imaginative eye, he evokes our childlike curiosity, taking us on a harrowing duck hunting expedition, ending in drop-dead wonder. Through detailed description we travel with Doyle into places now mostly forgotten in modern life and reexperience Nature's poetic embrace. Walking with Doyle through Hollister Ranch opens our instinctual intelligence. In his writings we rediscover Nature's eternal gift, a humanity rooted in the magnificence of the natural world."

— Stephen Aizenstat, Ph.D., founder and presiding chancellor of Pacifica Graduate Institute and author of *Dream Tending: Awakening to the Hidden Power of Dreams*

"Doyle Hollister writes from an unusual vantage point: In 1868 his great-grandfather William Welles Hollister acquired the vast tract that became Hollister Ranch, and Doyle experienced a free-range childhood there, exploring coves and canyons, riding horses and hunting deer, entranced by the wildness and wonder of it all.

"But great change was in store. In 1965, the family sold the ranch. For many years Doyle felt exiled—and heartbroken. After much searching he found a way back, returning with a deeper understanding of what the place means.

"Doyle reflects in rich detail upon the gifts of the great outdoors, and warns of the damage to the human spirit caused by the disconnection of contemporary life from the natural world. This is a book about the transformative powers of the land, the miracles it holds, and the profound grief that is unleashed by its loss. It is a love song to the ranch, and to the vital wilderness places of the earth."

—Cynthia Carbone Ward, author of *How Writers Grow* and *Getting There*

"This is more than a memoir; it is a love story. Through his evocative recounting of life on the Hollister Ranch, Doyle Hollister reveals in intimate detail that the spirits do indeed continue to abide in the land, calling us into relationship with its enduring presence, breaking our hearts, and opening us up to the mystery and power of place. As Doyle demonstrates, these are not theoretical ideas, but the real stuff of relationship: hard sacrifice and pure grace. Gratitude to Doyle for having the courage to feel so deeply, for remembering in spite of the pain, and ultimately for appeasing the spirits by returning to the center of his heart, the place which he now calls home. This book has much to offer anyone who has ever known a sense of place. Don't stop your longing. Let your heart break. No matter what happens to your place, no matter the gains or the losses, you will always remain connected, if you only dare to pay attention, remember, and most of all, risk falling even deeper in love."

—Betsy Perluss, MFT, Ph.D.,
School of Lost Borders guide,
Pacifica Graduate Institute faculty

"The writing flowing through the pages you're about to turn comes directly to you from the wilderness moving beautifully through this author. How does this happen—because the essence of a particular California ranchland is deeply interfused with the author's ancestors, history, and spirit.

"He invites you to walk with him as he remembers his roots in wilderness, where wind, fog, and manzanita sing together. We begin to feel the joy of that boy's ambles, so that when his family's ranch is sold and his contact with all that beauty ends, the eventual agonizing loss is deep enough to inspire a wild search for its retrieval.

"These pages help us remember Wordsworth's finding again his beloved hills; the resultant ascent of his spirit in poems of praise joins with Hollister's own gratitude for his boyhood's immersion and attunement to wind, darkness, and silence bonding him ever deeper with his landscape. As his readers we will then follow him into its utter loss, and then watch with hope as he, like Wordsworth, comes again to his own true hills waiting many years for his return."

—Michael Geis, MD, depth psychologist and poet

"Doyle Hollister grew up on the Hollister Ranch just below Point Conception on the Central California coast—a land sacred to the Chumash Indians who inhabited the area for thousands of years. It is largely protected today by the fact that the land is privately held with very limited development potential. In his memoir we experience Doyle's lifelong observations of the riches that this private wilderness holds for the fortunate few who live there. We discover the deep influences that Doyle's immersion in nature has had on his psyche.

"The reader also finds in Hollister's memoir how the history of this largely untrammeled landscape was threatened by a dangerous pipeline project that was to bring oil from offshore oil platforms to a multi-billion-dollar refinery. This story is emblematic of today's world, where no place is ever fully safe from the predations of oil development.

"Hollister describes the wonder of being a child of ten spending days alone in the wild, where Northern and Southern California's environments meet, intermingle, and sometimes clash with one another in titanic ways. The silence, deep darkness, and fierce winds, forces that would intimidate most young boys, come alive in us through Doyle's penetrating prose. The book is a little treasure of a memoir about a place most people will never see. Read it and you will experience the power of place in shaping a life."
—Paul Relis, founding director Community Environmental Council of Santa Barbara, author of *Out of the Wasteland: Stories from the Environmental Frontier*

"Doyle was raised by the wilderness nature of his family ranch, a boy free to adventure within the coastal and backcountry ensouled phenomena of nature. His memoir is a sensory testament of his love of the wilderness, reflecting on its importance to his physical, psychological, and spiritual development. He wonders out loud, on behalf of all of us: 'What is being lost when we lose our intimacy with nature and wilderness?' An authentic, moving story with implications for us all."
—Maren Hansen, M.Div., Ph.D., Pacifica Graduate Institute

"A careful naturalist, Doyle describes intimate experiences with the other—which invites us into the zen mind, a beginner mind that through the child soul discovers the elementals of the world beckoning. We are in no time and all time, where our experience of the primordial awakens. And we recognize the divine in nature in all things. It's delicious to wander into a family ranch life that offers daily communion with nature: to awaken to the spirit of wind, to enter into shape-shifting capacities with a tree, to be taken into the energy of windswept waves or the ecosystem in a tidal pool, experience the wild comfort of the searing night sky, and to be held at the dire mercy of a thunderstorm. Doyle's natural voice and unassuming way allows the reader to easily join him in the experiences. And in so doing, his work may reintroduce us to the appetite within ourselves for this nourishing experiential ever available relationship with the nature gods, and the greater Tao.

"For some, this read will be a remembering and rediscovering of our deepest loves; for others it may be somewhat like a survival map—if you've never tasted such depth of solitude with the soul and natural world, you likely will be drawn into it now. It is a remarkable journey into the refuge of peace that can be discovered in the company of wild things. His work will likely change you, for Doyle Hollister's offering carries a powerful healing antidote with its capacity to open individual consciousness as well as a ripple effect into the far beyond."

—Monika Wikman, Ph.D., Jungian analyst,
author of *Pregnant Darkness and the Rebirth of Consciousness*

I Only Went Out for a Walk

I Only Went
Out for a Walk

*Finding My Wilderness Soul
on a California Ranch*

Doyle Hollister

2018 · DOS CUERVOS
MONTECITO, CALIFORNIA

ISBN 978-1-7320274-0-4

Published by Dos Cuervos
1187 Coast Village Road, #146
Montecito, CA, 93108

The author gratefully acknowledges permission to reprint the following:

"The great sea" by Uvavnuk [p. 193: 6 I.] from *Women in Praise of the Sacred*, edited by Jane Hirshfield. Copyright © 1994 by Jane Hirshfield. Reprinted by permission of HarperCollins Publishers.

Excerpt from "The Answer"
The Collected Poetry of Robinson Jeffers, Volume 2: 1928–1938 by Robinson Jeffers, edited by Tim Hunt. Copyright © 1989 by Jeffers Literary Properties. Reprinted by permission.

Excerpt from "Invasion"
The Collected Poetry of Robinson Jeffers, Volume 3: 1939–1962 by Robinson Jeffers, edited by Tim Hunt. Copyright © 1977 by Jeffers Literary Properties. Reprinted by permission.

William Stafford, excerpts from "Wind World" from *The Darkness Around Us Is Deep: Selected Poems*. Copyright © 1973 by William Stafford. Reprinted with the permission of The Permissions Company, Inc. on behalf of Kim Stafford.

"This Poem Is for Deer (Hunting 8)" By Gary Snyder, from MYTHS AND TEXTS, copyright ©1978 by Gary Snyder. Reprinted by permission of New Directions Publishing Corp.

"To Know the Dark" from *Farming: A Hand Book* by Wendell Berry. Copyright © 1971, 2011 by Wendell Berry. Reprinted by permission of Counterpoint Press.

The Practice of the Wild by Gary Snyder. Copyright © 1990 by Gary Snyder. Reprinted by permission of Counterpoint Press.

"I talk to my inner lover…" by Kabir, translated by Robert Bly. From *Kabir: Try to Live to See This!* 9th publication 1986.

To the twins, Jane and Clinty,

and to my wife, Joanne, for decades of patience

Acknowledgments

My gratitude extends out to many: to Jo, John, and Linda Wheelwright, as without their embrace supporting Jane's, I would still be lost; to Betty Wheelwright, who upon a raw first read of this work a decade ago said, "Well, you have something here, I just don't know what"; to Cynthia Carbone Ward, whose interview and editing lit the fire to finish after years of stalling; to Eric Larson of Studio E Books for his love of nature, humor, guidance, and frank talk, all assisting the formal final publication; to Rick Sawyer for his mussels and photography; to Derek Mast for accompanying me across the technological finish line; to Bendy White for running over the ice chest and for deeply understanding the importance of my journey; to cousin Charlie Ramsburg for weeping in the back of my truck within his resonant reconnection ranch moment; to Stan Witnov, Movement Man, for his friendship and support of Mountain Man; to Ivor John and his deep passion and love for "wind"; to my beautiful children, Kyle and Ashley, for sharing my love for the land and wanting our ranch heritage to continue; to the grandchildren, Stella, Theo, and Hannah, the next generation, for the purity of their childhood interest in lizards, frogs, and sea shells; and to my wife, Joanne, for her thirty-four-year support of my quest and ongoing courage to now live in the wilderness of Tepitates, "the sacred high place," our home.

Contents

Foreword

THE TRADITION of European Romanticism in the 18th and 19th centuries offered, both in its poetry and philosophy of Nature, a compensation for the rapidly developing goals, assumptions, and capabilities of the scientific revolution. Whereas the scientific mind sought to understand and overcome nature through causal analysis and dialectical materialism, separating out mind from body and mind from matter, the Romantics envisioned a world in which mind and nature were inseparably locked in a mutual embrace. "Spousal verse" was how Wordsworth described his poetry, referring to just that, the creative relatedness between soul and world. Whereas the progenitors of the European Enlightenment tended to regard imagination as tantamount to irreality, and stripped Nature bare of human imagination that it might be seen objectively for how it is, the Romantics valued imagination as world-creative—"in our life alone does Nature live," Coleridge wrote. Whereas the trajectory of human development for the Enlightenment was an arrow pointed straight up into the future ("progress"), the Romantics envisioned themselves and their culture to be on a circuitous journey in which separation and alienation from the self and the world was a necessary stage along the way in the greater journey towards conscious wholeness.

If I had to place Doyle Hollister's very personal book within a larger cultural context I would pick Romanticism. Shimmering with poetic description that paints vividly heartfelt stories of connection between imagination and nature, Doyle's writing, like that of the Romantics who came before, is a compensation for a technological society that we and our children are increasingly caught up in, perhaps even unconsciously addicted to.

Wordsworth's epic poem, his masterpiece, is "The Prelude," which is subtitled "Growth of a Poet's Mind." In this poem Wordsworth tracks his psychological development from childhood, particularly focusing on the role that Nature, and his experiences of communion with Nature as a child, played in his psychological development. The growth of a poet's mind—for both Wordsworth and Hollister—necessarily involves loss and painful alienation from childhood merger experiences with nature, and conscious steps taken through creativity (for example writing *The Prelude*, or *I Only Went Out for a Walk*) to circle back again to those merger experiences as an adult. Placed within Doyle's decades long work as a therapist, his writing gives weight to the theory that personal relationship is not the only factor in human development. Solitude, in Doyle's amazing stories, is not isolation but communion, relationship, an opening through which the archetypal imagination comes alive and carries him towards an unknown goal that only becomes visible in hindsight, the goal of the self. Not a nostalgic wish to return to childhood, *I Only Went Out for a Walk* is a mature reflection on the ways in which a contemporary adult with one foot planted firmly in Western civilization, raising a family, creating a full time practice as a Marriage Family therapist, paying taxes and saving money for retirement, using technology all the time in his everyday life, might at the same time also be allowed to circle back again to the wild self and value the role it played, and continues to play, in the "Growth of a Poet's Mind."

I write this on the day that SpaceX launched Falcon Heavy, the world's most powerful rocket, into space on its maiden voyage. About four minutes after launch, heading out into deep space, the rocket jettisoned a white nose cone, revealing its payload: Elon Musk's Tesla Roadster with "Starman," a mannequin astronaut, in the driver's seat. Perhaps Starman is a symbol, an expression of the possibility that we may ourselves leave the earth in the near future and take our civilization into space, never to return, the image of the trajectory of the Western mind. Contemporary technology is so stunning, so truly awesome, that it has co-opted the words "future" and "progress." Yet, if you can even for a second imagine Doyle Hollister seated next to Starman in a space-bound Tesla roadster then you do not know Doyle. Doyle's writing draws a line pulling down on Starman's upward flight, a tension pulling down and back again, drawn down by love for the human experience of Earth.

Perhaps those who do not climb aboard in the Tesla next to Starman will prove in time to belong to the past and to regression. But perhaps not. The hidden questions that haunt Doyle haunt many people today. Have we have lost something essential to our humanity through our culture's one-sided identification with technological progress? If so, can we find it again? Is it possible to marry the civilized with the indigenous mind and by doing so not leave the earth but recreate our experience of self and world? In merger with the natural world, Mother becomes the territory of earth, wind, and sea that speaks to Doyle and nurtures him. Doyle's amazing and beautiful stories offer us his personal experiences, if not answers, to questions that many of us may also find gnawing from within. As we read these stories, we may find again the value of being a human animal in a natural habitat—not an "environment" but a home that is made soulful by the experience of soul within it.

—Thomas Elsner,
J.D., M.A, Jungian analyst

I Only Went Out for a Walk

The Dream

The great sea
frees me, moves me
as a strong river carries a weed.
Earth and her strong winds
move me, take me away
and my soul is swept up in joy.

—Eskimo woman shaman, Uvavnuk,
in *Women in Praise of the Sacred*

THE DREAM THAT INITIATED the flood of words came to me one late morning, just before I awoke and rose for the day. Dreams at that time are often very lucid. They can have strong emotions to them, and they linger. So it was with this one. It began with a flickering image of myself as a young boy, around the age of ten, with my family—my father, mother, brother, and friends—enjoying a day at Bulito Canyon beach, the main beach for our family on the old Hollister ranch. We did not frequent the beach. We spent much more time in the backcountry. When we did go to the beach, there were a few regular activities we engaged in, one of which was to play, wade, swim in, and explore the large slough, which formed an estuary between the canyon's creek and the ocean. It was there that the reflection in my dream occurred.

In the dream we were dallying in the estuary and ocean as usual, when I had a moment of greater awareness. I sensed that

21

all that was happening there with my family in this beautiful landscape was unique, a very special time. It was as if I were two people now, one young boy enjoying a normal day at the beach, and another boy standing in the background observing and reflecting on the meaning of the moment. The feeling that accompanied this image and realization was profound. I felt a deep sense of joy, an exuberance, almost ecstasy.

My perspective then switched as I turned around, still in this altered state, and began to look up the coastline. The family and the slough faded into the background, and I found myself somewhere around Bulito Point, all alone, walking west along the beach toward Cojo Canyon, the last canyon on our ranch. It was not clear where I was, but what was clear was that I was all alone. The feeling was still elation, but now there was an underlying peacefulness. I felt that I had returned to a very important experience in my life, one in which I was walking by myself, all alone, far from family and friends, in the wilderness here the beach, yet not feeling lonely at all. Quite the contrary, I felt distinctly serene, joyous, and complete.

The dream lingered for some time. I was profoundly immersed in the moment of my coastal walk in dreamtime. Then I woke up. But still the strong euphoric sensation continued as I lay in bed drifting into reflections of the many times I had walked all alone along the ranch coastline as a young boy.

I contemplated the fact that for most people the experience of walking along a coastline is probably a unique encounter with self and nature. It is a sensual realm: the constant sound of the surf breaking in the background of consciousness; the wind whistling caressingly past the ear; the soft, dry sand that squeaks when one's foot rubs across the surface; the cool, moist sand just abandoned by the outgoing tide; the pungent scent of fresh kelp left on the beach by a storm; perhaps the stinging windblown sand painfully pricking one's ankles on a breezy day; maybe even the magnificent sight of offshore windblown surf with spray that flies off the tops of the breaking waves and freckles the water behind with sparkling sunlit beads. All of these capture the mind and body in a special way when on walks on any beach.

But what crashed through into my awareness from my dream was the absolute pristine solitude of such moments, and the rapture that came with the realization that I was totally alone. Yes, family may have been three or four miles away; but other than them there was not a soul for fifteen to twenty miles. In this solitude I felt a mix of fear and excitement: the fear of being completely alone in the wild, and the excitement of the same. Occasionally I would come across a sea lion camouflaged in the massive mounds of kelp on the beach, and the sudden movement of such a large mammal, with its immediate barking, would send my heart and adrenaline system flying for a minute or so. But that was the extent of the physical threat. The real fear or threat came from within myself: my age, my solitude, my isolation, and the direct contact with the wild. But paradoxically it was the seduction of this wild that lured me to wander farther, around the next point, to experience what I might experience, wilderness unknown.

Lying in bed that morning after the dream, I began to realize how absolutely spellbound I was by the beauty of the coastal environment: the blue-green color of the sea, the formations of pelican gliding silently by, the spontaneous sculptures of white sand dunes, the tan-white shale cliffs crumbling down to the sand surface, and high on those cliffs the mud nests of swallows like Anasazi cave dwellings, and the small sand cliffs left by the ebbing tide. Beauty on and on. I thought that at my age then I wouldn't have described what I beheld as beautiful; it was simply exciting to my young soul. I began to consider that something very important had happened to me in those times wandering alone on the beach and in other wild places on the ranch. This solitude and unfettered contact with nature had mentored me into a person with deep understanding and appreciation of wilderness beauty. A person was being formed as I grew up interacting with ranch wilderness, a person nurtured and matured by nature in an extraordinary way.

This mentoring by nature could never have occurred with people around. It happened because of the purity of my aloneness. With nobody around for miles, adaptive social stances simply were not needed. With no boundary between the natural surroundings and myself, wilderness could be directly, purely, and freely experienced and absorbed. The combination of this unfiltered contact with nature, the freedom within solitude, and the instinctual child's mind created a world and an experience that might be described as indigenous, even feral. In this primitive state of being, life was experienced quite differently from urban experience. There was a wisdom offered by wild nature that was very different from whatever wisdom one might acquire in society.

Eventually, after this very moving dream and the subsequent reflections, I thought it might be interesting to explore more thoroughly what occurred as I grew up on the ranch. Beyond that, it might be interesting to explore the entire story of growing up in wilderness, then losing this landed heritage completely for a decade and a half, and ultimately reuniting with my childhood wilderness as an adult. I thought it would be valuable for me to understand this better, and perhaps it would be interesting to others as well.

Thus I began to write, and the outcome is this work. It is raw in its expression, but then the whole experience was raw. Many times the words have come from a surge of emotions and reflections that had a life of their own. In a sense, writing has been like walking up the coastline or some other wild part of the ranch, wandering off into the unknown not knowing what was to happen. I have tried to shape the results into a coherent whole. It has been divided into two parts, childhood and adolescent memories of growing up on the ranch, followed by the years of disconnect and the early years of reconnection that culminated in reuniting with the land as an adult. The remembering and writing has been an immensely enjoyable endeavor for me. I hope others may experience the same. The journey begins.

PART I

Childhood Memories

My heart leaps up when I behold
  A rainbow in the sky:
So it was when my life began;
So it is now I am a man;
So be it when I shall grow old,
  Or let me die!
The Child is father of the Man;
And I could wish my days to be
Bound each to each by natural piety.

—William Wordsworth, 1779–1850

Santa Anita:
Power of Place

*As humans, we also require support for our spirits,
and this is what certain kinds of places provide. The
catalyst that converts any physical location—any environment if you will—into a place, is the process of
experiencing deeply. A place is a piece of the whole
environment that has been claimed by feeling*

—Alan Gussow, *A Sense of Place:
The Artist and the American Land*

THOUGH EACH WILDERNESS PLACE has power unique to
itself, whether it be the mesmerizing beauty of the ocean waves
breaking on gray-white sandy shores, the still serenity of the
flatlands, or the tumultuous energy of the wild California backcountry, nothing has more power than wilderness places where
some life experience has occurred. When something has been
experienced at a specific location, that place, now embued with
memory and story, becomes what Native Americans referred to
as a place of power in one's personal history with the land, and
that place takes on much more meaning. Having been blessed
with thousands of acres of wilderness to roam for most of my
childhood, I can now, as an elder in my sixties, wander about
the ranch and be filled with lucid memories of experiences specifically connected to certain places. The memories involved
are crystal clear and can invoke all the sensory experiences that

went with the original moments. Though there are myriads of places on the ranch that have power for me, one stands out in particular, as it was also the place where my grief, in response to my eventual loss of the land, flooded my life after a decade and a half of denial and complete disconnection.

This particular place of power was the area around the Santa Anita Canyon slough, where the large canyon's creek reached the ocean shore. Santa Anita Canyon is a spectacular canyon in every way. It is a wide and winding canyon that was second only to Bulito Canyon with regard to its use by our family and ranch hands. Its best asset was the water that came from a perennial creek that could be followed from its outlet at the sea to the neighboring San Julian Ranch on the other side of the coastal mountain range. But the specific power spot for me was the slough, where the creek finalized its journey. The slough and its surroundings were rich in wildlife and environmental variety. The beach, cupped by a beautiful small bay, was protected by very similar and dramatic shale promontories on each end. Swallows would build their mud nests precariously on the steepest upper parts of these cliffs. The slough and beach area seemed to join together in a joint endeavor to collect an abundance of driftwood, which would settle around the edges of the slough itself. The ever-changing ecosystem here, where salt and fresh water mixed, always negotiating their eternal marriage, made for a rich gathering of shorebirds, ducks, pelicans, seagulls, herons, and egrets. The slough itself was always changing its depth and width, and as such was a constant source of intrigue to a young boy. There was also a dark and foreboding tunnel that allowed the creek water to flow under a man-made earthen railroad embankment. The dark, moist alluring tunnel was a world of mystery, and its temptation added immensely to the allure of the area. Then there was the train, a man-made entity that day and night would burst thunderously into one's awareness when one least expected it, breaking one's entranced state of mind.

So it was at this particular place, the Santa Anita slough, that my brother, friends, and I would seek adventure for weekends at a time. The experience would begin even before we got there, as getting there was an adventure in itself. Our usual means of travel was either by foot or, in later years, in a glorified go-cart built on a chassis like that of a Model-T Ford, and powered by a Briggs and Straton lawnmower engine. If we were careful we could fit three persons in this vehicle and, holding our guns and sleeping bags, we would take off into the darkness of some promising night, using flashlights for headlights, directing ourselves excitedly toward the Santa Anita slough.

The travel was always a source of some anxiety, since it was always possible that the little car would not get us there. But the real excitement began when we arrived. We grew up in a hunting community, and so the focus of our endeavor was to wake up early in the morning and strategically plan a hunt for the wild ducks that often stopped in the slough on their migratory travels. When (and if) we arrived at Santa Anita, we carefully parked the little car on the opposite side of the ridge from the slough. Then, with all our gear in hand, we quietly and slowly stole our way over the ridge, down through the mustard stalks and various brush patches, working our way down to what we referred to as the "elephant grass," a rich, thick, bulbous grass that grew about fifty yards above the water line of the slough. The grass was our mattress and was extremely comfortable as we lay on top of it in our sleeping bags.

Here we would situate ourselves, roll out our sleeping bags, tuck our guns under the bags to keep off moisture, then snuggle in and wait for dawn and the hunt. The night, however, was always filled with wonder, excitement, and threat, so much so that we hardly slept. There was excitement in just being miles away from our house, tucked in the warm sleeping bags, listening to the wild sounds of the night. We could hear the ducks in the slough below, quacking occasionally, then flapping their wings against the surface of the water. There was always the soothing symphony of frogs, whose serenade only ceased when some larger animal moved through the area. Should that happen, along with any crackling of twigs nearby, our young bodies would surge with fear, as we imagined a possible confrontation with something big and wild in the blackness of the night.

Then there was the train. In the middle of the noisy silence of night, as we lay in this wilderness somewhere between the real world and the dream world, we began to hear the distant rumbling of the train, as it wound down the coastline like a giant metallic snake. We were usually about thirty yards from the train tracks, and the trestle elevation was about the same distance above us. The canyon walls muffled the sound of the approaching train, so that the train would seem to burst out of the darkness, startling us with its metallic clamor and bright roving light. It thundered in our ears and throughout our bodies as the air and ground vibrated with the train's movement. The brilliant intensity of the train's light, a cyclops-like beam that roamed from side to side, seemed like the voracious, vacuous eye of a one-eyed snake, searching in the night for something to eat. Though there was absolutely no danger at all in the train's passing, terror overcame us for that brief yet seemingly eternal moment in time as this man-made metallic monster rammed its reality into the silence of nature's night. The train always passed and, though it was exciting to behold, we felt relief when it wound its way into the distance and we could return to the much more subtle excitement of the nighttime natural wilderness.

Though it often seemed interminable, the night eventually passed. As the subtle early morning light emerged from the

darkness, our excitement increased in a different way as we antic-
ipated the morning hunt. There was much talk about what kind
of ducks there might be out there. This was a wonderful part of
the hunt, as it was filled with reverence for wildlife. There was an
implicit hierarchy among the waterfowl. The mallard, specifically
the male mallard or green head, was at the top of the hierarchy.
Of nearly equal prestige was the pintail or sprig. Both the latter
were uncommon, so whenever we found them the hunt became
even more magical, as not only were they beautiful and rare, they
were extremely intelligent, and more often than not they would
outsmart us. If there were not mallards or sprigs, there might be
blue-winged, green-winged, or cinnamon teal. Or, on the lower
end of the hierarchy, there might be a surf scooter, a salt- and
fresh-water duck. Regardless of what was there, once we had
peered through the mustard stalks and scoped out where the
promising ducks were, we would begin making intricate strate-
gies. We would go to any length to get good position from which
to surprise the ducks. Extensive crawling on the ground through
the brush and elaborate hand signals were all part of the hunt.
It was extremely exciting, and when someone was actually successful it was deeply satisfying to all involved. It is true, though,
that when someone got one of the ducks of hierarchal prestige,
a tinge of envy would arise among the others.

Though the hunt was the most actively exhilarating experience of our time at the Santa Anita slough, the rest of the day
also had a solid contribution to making this location a power
place. I have a photograph on my office wall today of Apache
men in the wilderness. They are gathered together, some standing and some sitting, while one of them, with a stick in hand, is
showing and telling something to the others. The photograph is
titled "Story Telling." That is what we would do. A fire would be
made from whatever driftwood we could gather, each of us would
recount our personal adventure during the morning's hunt, and

we would recall stories about the night before and the interesting sounds we had heard in the dark.

The day would progress from this storytelling into a variety of activities, all of which had a drifting, trance-like quality to them. There might be more hunting or fire-making, or beach or tunnel exploring, or driftwood structure building, or raft building, all done in a spontaneous and natural way, simply wandering and relating to the elements of the wilderness. It would be a full day of activity, extending into late afternoon or early evening. Then, eventually, our active young bodies would wind down into a sleepy fatigue, and we gathered our guns and bags, climbed aboard the little car, and headed back, tired young kids, to Bulito Canyon, family, and friends. I remember always feeling satiated with adventure as I drifted through dreamy reflections of all that we did on any particular occasion at the Santa Anita slough. It felt like a night and day well spent.

However, as I write this now, decades later, in the back of my mind I am disappointed to hear my own adolescent children telling me that the reason they don't want to go to the ranch more often is that there just isn't that much to do. This turns my head around in surprise and bewilderment, in a slap of astonishment. Nothing to do at the ranch? What? There was *always* something to do at the Santa Anita slough, endless adventures. On the other hand, I can't fault my children. They didn't grow up with thousands of acres as their back yard. They didn't have such an intimate relationship with this land in such a free, unsupervised, and wild way. They are the norm. I am the one who is odd in having had an intimate relationship with the land from such a young and impressionable age. I struggle hard to put these things in perspective, yet I am always left somewhat disturbed.

A lingering question haunts me. What are my children— indeed, what are *all* children losing by not having an intimate relationship with nature? What is lost if children do not experience a particular place in nature that holds the significance of a power place, as the Santa Anita slough did for me? When I closed my eyes, falling asleep on Sunday night after a weekend adventure at the slough, I would see in my mind's eye the beautiful symmetry of a duck's flight pattern as it approached its landing over the bronze and green colored reeds, wings straight out, webbed feet outstretched, gliding softly onto the glassy water, leaving a small wake on the water behind. I would fall asleep to images of birds, animals, sunrises and sunsets, and a deep feeling of wholeness and substance, a body and mind at peace. Reflecting back now, I can see that I fell asleep feeling more secure as a young person, though at the time I would not have described it that way. Back then I just felt really good, tired, and ready for sleep as these wild images danced in my head, soothing the dread of having to go back to school the next day.

I see that my young soul was being fed continuously by the timeless imagery of the ranch wilderness, and that these images connected me to a primal level of experience that has fortified my life in some mysterious but essential way. Bricks were being laid in the platform of my young evolving life. Even as I sit here now, recounting memories at the Santa Anita slough, I feel more complete as a grown man because of that reflection. That place nurtured me and raised me, and I feel grateful and blessed for having had those wonderful experiences of power and place at such an early age. And so I cannot help asking myself, with heartfelt concern, what images are our children falling asleep to, and where are their personal places of power?

Wind

Wind world likes it near
The ground, and hurries there
Even on still days, low,
You can see him shaking hands
With himself in the grass.

Wind world likes things that
Move, but you notice
He has to pass something still
For him to really sing a song.

—William Stafford, "Wind World," in
The Darkness Around Us Is Deep

WIND IS REALLY NOT that interesting on its own, merely air moving across the earth's surface. In the city, wind is less than uninteresting; it is bothersome, and when the air is *really* moving across the earth's surface, it can be dangerous and terrifying. In the city it is never exhilarating in a positive way. But when one moves from the city to the wilderness, the wind interacts with all of what is on the earth's surface in nature, and it can be a magical phenomenon in many ways.

On the ranch, wind was almost a daily experience. The spirit of a wind varies according to where one experiences it. As children, we wandered throughout the day most of the time. Our

wanderings could take us anywhere from the beach to the top
of the coastal range mountains. So we experienced the wind
in different places all the time. It became a kind of wilderness
companion.

THE wind usually came up late in the afternoon, close to sunset. The houses on the ranch were protected by eucalyptus trees
planted by the family decades ago. These trees were strategically
placed in rows to break the wind, or placed in forest-like groves,
protective clusters. The ones that lined the roads like sentries
were sources of great entertainment in the wind. First of all, the
noise of the wind as it blew the long, sleek, rather stiff, green
eucalyptus leaves was absolutely exquisite, a hissing sound when
a very strong gust hit the tree. The wind would intensify, and
suddenly the line of trees would emit a loud noise, and one's
consciousness, wherever it may have been, would be drawn to
these sentinels along the way.

On one such occasion, drawn to the roaring sound of wind
in the trees, and attracted by the flickering light on the glossy
leaves in the golden sunset, we wondered what it would be like to
be up in a tree in the wind. So we each chose a tree, and climbed
up as far as we could. Creeping up the eucalyptus trunks, limb by
limb, each of us managed to climb quite a way up, high enough
to have a panoramic view all around. The wind got stronger and
stronger, and the trees, tall, straight, and slender, swayed wildly
with the movement of the air. From the ground it's hard to tell
how much the upper portions of a tree move, but when you're
clinging to the upper level of a tree trunk, you become aware of
a substantial sway back and forth.

So there we were, high up in these arboreal sentinels, pro-
tectors of the domestic domain, fearfully embracing the trunks
of the trees, their leaves flickering, hissing, and sparkling in the
wind and sun all around us, swaying back and forth, looking out

over the landscape bathed in the golden rose light of the setting sun. We were completely immersed in these trees. There is nothing quite like being immersed in anything. Immersion is truly a way to comprehensively understand a thing that one really wants to understand, giving one an empathetic perspective on what it is like to be whatever one is immersed in.

Prior to climbing the trees, I had not really wondered what it might be like to be a tree. But high up in those eucalyptus trees in the strong wind, my young imagination got a real sense of "treeness." It was as if the wind brought out the full experience of what a tree is. I began to understand how tough their job of protecting us was, as they struggled against the wind, their trunks swaying back and forth in this give-and-take battle, creaking, almost moaning in this movement, a seeming expression of the effort involved. As a sudden and prolonged blast of wind came through, I became aware that the tree could be defeated by the wind. The wind could snap its body in two or uprooting its base, and throw it onto the ground in submission and defeat.

However, despite this flight of imagination and immersion, my concern for the tree's welfare was soon clouded by my more immediate concern for myself. So as the wind increased its foray to an even higher level, sending the leaves into a deafening rustle and vibrant shimmering, we all decided to climb down, leaving the trees to their own difficult task, unfettered by our boyish interference.

At the time, it seemed that the wind was much the stronger force. But now, decades later, seeing that all of those trees are still standing, I am inclined to think of the interaction between wind and tree as an ongoing dance between the two. It seems like play rather than strife. Well, perhaps it is a little of both. One thing is absolutely true though, and that is the exhilarating memory I retain of those moments immersed in tree, wind, and dusk. It was a great place to be at the end of a day, and I must be thankful to the wind for giving me this moment in which I could experience, as close as I might, what it must be like to actually be a tree.

WIND at the beach is a very different thing from wind in the trees. The beach always seemed to call me to walk alone long distances, to stray from whatever group I might be with, and wander alone up or down the coast. The wind would often be my companion on these coastline ambulations. Although most of my experiences of wind at the beach were positive, one that was at the very best an ambivalent experience was wind carrying the sand along the surface the beach. Though wind-borne sand could look romantically like phantoms swirling low along the peppered terrain, when these infinitesimally small particles hit bare skin, it was as if thousands of pinpoints were striking one's lower legs and ankles all at once. This pain would send me wildly running, lifting my legs as high as possible to escape the attack, my destination being the wet sand, unmovable by the wind, a welcome relief.

However, aside from the meditation-breaking experience of stinging sand, the wind at the beach was transfixing. One of the most beautiful wilderness visions was the wind's interplay with large surf. As I walked along, enveloped by the sound of surf and the smells of salt air and seaweed, the wind lifting water off the top of a breaking wave with the sun setting in the background made a breathtakingly glorious spectacle. The water, lifting off the wave just as the wave broke into white foam, could travel thirty to forty feet back out to sea. This was a vision my mind and imagination would simply never grow tired of witnessing. The beauty of this wind–sea ballet was relentless. My imagination seemed to call forth an image of myriads of sea maidens approaching the shore all at once, immersed in the waves, having traveled thousands of nautical miles and now, finally, coming to rest on the white sands of this coastline. Their heads, emerging from the blue-green water, were met by the offshore wind moving across the ocean's surface, their hair blown straight back, clearing their vision for the last part of the journey, the merging with the coastline terrain, *terra durra*. With this image before me, along with the symphony of waves breaking and the wind sounding in ear, the pungent smell of the salt-water world in nose, my mind would drift into some timeless experiential domain, which is still with me in my reflections. The wind, the wizard at the center, creates a moment that is as close to an experience of the eternal as I can imagine, a deep sense of being related to all things beyond the confines of space and time, someplace ancient and forever, infinite. And it is the wind that is at the helm of this moment of magic.

THE wind can create a similar unique and exhilarating experience at the other end of the physical world, the world of the backcountry, the world of sandstone, manzanita, and tanbark oak, the central California coastal mountain range ridgetop. In the ranch backcountry the wind could be especially ferocious, and it brought a variety of different experiences with it. My most prominent recollection is of the strength and power of the ridgetop air moving across earth's surface. As young boys, when we encountered intense winds on these ridges, we would find a large protruding sandstone rock, usually facing north, looking out panoramically over the inland valley. We would climb to the top of the rock, towering over even the tall tanbark trees, and lean into the oncoming wind. It was like standing in the middle of river rapids, only this was air power, not water power. We could literally lean out over the rock with confidence that we would not fall straight down onto the rock below. We would lean into the wind and hover, much like hawks hover, heads down, statuesque, scanning the ground for prey. It would give me the sensation of what it might be like to be one of those wind-borne birds, the red-tailed hawk, the turkey vulture, even the condor that once frequented this range. The air thundering past my ear, leaning, leaning more and more, fielding the bursts of greater intensity winds, arms outstretched, hair blown straight back, the biting chill cold on my face, eyes watering, leaning, leaning over the vertical drop, scanning the terrain, hovering, balancing, adjusting moment to moment to the ever-shifting currents, I was the red-tailed hawk. Again, I was immersed in the ridgetop wind world experience; I was one of the creatures that inhabit this wild wind world, out of myself and into some other world and some other way of being, a magical and exhilarating transformation. And, again, the wind was the wizard behind it all.

There were other wind experiences on the ridgetop, when the wind was not as intense. One that stands out in my memory and is still a frequent experience today is wind on the ridge when the inland fog moved in, blanketing the manzanita and tanbark oaks. The softer wind was mesmerizing in its own way. As the air moved across the earth's surface here, caressing the tops of the manzanitas and the branches of the tanbark oaks, there was a full, constant, soft, and lulling hum that captured one's consciousness entrancingly. The manzanita had a thick and strong stalk, a polished rusty bronze color, and the leaves inhabited only the uppermost part of the plant. The abundance of this plant on the ridgetop created a parapet five to ten feet above the ground and hollow below. When the wind caressed the tops of these plants the resulting sound was similar to the sonorous drone of ocean waves breaking in the distance. When the inland fog was added to the experience, the combination created a magnificent mood. The ghostly white vapor floated, wind powered, over the ridgetop with the background sound of the manzanita parapet humming. The fog saddled the ridge in its movement, hit the subtle ocean-side updraft from a deep canyon and did a back-flip swirl as the two air currents collided—again, all to the lulling sound of the air moving across the earth's surface atop the manzanita. The mood this set was spellbinding. It was a solitary mood, in my experience, one that seemed to remind me that I was really alone in the world in some ultimate or absolute way. But it was not, and still is not, a lonely sensation. It was an experience of being alone and being full inside, having a home within the isolation. Words are difficult in these moments, as the experience was really somewhere beyond words. But I recall times when all alone and miles away from any friend or family member, I walked along those ridgetops, wind, fog, and manzanita singing together. Something character-building was happening, something soul-building was rumbling inside of me as I experienced this landscape. And, once again, the wind, that air moving across the earth's surface, was and is the deep power behind it all.

Last but not least, one other tree that is especially sonorous when played by the wind is the splendid and multitudinous oak. Though there are many species of oak in California, approximately nineteen, the one that was most frequently encountered on the ranch was the coast live oak. These trees nestled themselves in the mid-canyon zone, which was the section of the ranch between the backcountry ridgetop sandstone and the lower, more open rolling hill-and-flatland section of the ranch near the ocean. They clustered in the lower portions of the canyon where there was often a small creek. All of the canyons had roads that wound between those oak groves. The architecture of those old oaks was magnificent. The trees were dense round helmets of leaves richly dark green in color, and this helmet of leaves was supported by the twisted gray sculpture of gnarled trunks and branches. Each tree had its own personality in the unique formation that the mysterious branching beauty took. Not particularly tall trees, they often spread out parallel to the earth almost as wide as they were tall, a rambling branch life.

Those trees were wondrous entities of life in themselves,

but again when the wind commenced its interchange with those oak tree groves, the result was magnificent. I can remember countless times returning home after an evening's hunt, walking through the trees in the early darkness. Although they were quiet and stationary arboreal sculptures during the day, at night, as the wind howled through them, they made an unbelievably stimulating world. The voluminous and comprehensive sound of wind-shaken oak limbs resounding in the night would stop me in my tracks in a state of complete awe and inspiration. It was a startling and all-encompassing sound; nothing could be heard above that surging noise, it was so loud and close. It could be frightening in a beautiful way. I can remember debating whether to pick up my pace so as to escape the noise into the more open treeless lower portion of the canyon, or to stop, stand still, and courageously embrace the moment. Usually I responded with a move somewhere in between. Eventually I emerged from the oak groves of the narrow wind-blown canyon, and the contrast with the open valley made it even more clear how loud and intense the oaks and wind were.

Although my experiences with wind are very special to me, I can't say that others have the same response. One of my friends who had experienced life on the ranch said that for him wind was just irritating, a complete bother. He hated it. Everybody is different. For me, wind created magical events. Air in motion, interplayed with various other elements of the ranch wilderness, became a magician that brought forth unique sounds and images, new and different kinds of beauty, created out of the more common beauty of the land. Perhaps those reading this chapter might notice the world differently the next time they encounter wind, moving across earth's surface in the wild. If this be so, enjoy...

The Storm

Come out of your warm, angular house, resounding with
few voices, into the chill, grand, instantaneous night,
with such a Presence as a full moon in the clouds, and
you are struck with poetic wonder.

—Ralph Waldo Emerson, *Journals*

IT WAS MY FATHER'S IDEA to take the family camping, a
change from the usual routine. Normally, family and friends
would spend weekends at what was referred to as "the Hotel."
This was a big ranch-style house with about eight bedrooms that
could comfortably house twenty people. My father wanted to do
something different, however, and why not? It was the summer-
time, about mid-August, and it was his desire to round up the
usual families and have all the men, women, and children camp
up in the east fork of Bulito Canyon in a beautiful willow tree
glen that hid a natural spring, a perfect place for a camp-out.
Though it really took some coaxing of the women, especially
my mother, they all succumbed to the pressure and agreed to
give it a try.

The Jeeps were loaded up with sleeping bags, food, and
rifles, as it was deer season and the men wanted to go hunting the next day. We brought no tents because the weather had
been beautiful, and sleeping out under the stars at that elevation, away from electric lights of any kind for miles, would give

us a spectacularly clear view of the stars filling the summer sky. Although the camp site was not far from the Hotel as the crow flies, the road meandered up the canyon so tortuously that the camp was about five miles by car from any shelter. There were no paved roads up the canyons, but in mid-summer the clay soil was hard and dry, and facilitated access without need of four-wheel drive.

So up the canyon we all went in the soft, warm early evening air, lit by the golden beams of the westering sun. It was one of those evenings when there was absolutely no wind, not even a slight breeze, an unusually still, warm summer evening, quiet and serene. There were about fifteen of us in all. The evening was relaxed and uneventful. Some people hunted, some hiked, some made dinner. We all ate, and shortly after that everyone drifted to their sleeping bags, lay out on the dry summer grass in the warm night air, and drifted off into some manner of sleep.

It must have been about 2:00 A.M. that the rain came, seemingly out of nowhere. It was preceded by some foreboding flashes of lightning and distant thunder. Then bit by bit, the lightning and thunder grew closer together until they were almost simultaneous. Then, astonishing to everyone given the earlier evening weather, we found ourselves right in the middle of a thunderstorm.

"Thunderstorm: A transient storm of lightning and thunder, usually with rain and gusty winds, sometimes with hail and snow, produced by cumulonimbus clouds in which localized centers of electrical charge have developed." "Lightning: A luminous electrical discharge or crash between the upper positive center and the lower negative center produced in thunderstorm clouds." "Thunder: A loud, explosive, resounding noise produced by the explosive expansion of air heated by a lightning discharge." "Cumulonimbus: A cloud of a class indicative of thunderstorm conditions, characterized by large, dense, and very tall towers, cumuliform except for their tops, which appear fibrous because of the presence of ice crystals; occurs as a single cloud or as a group with merged basis and separate tops, often referred to as weather factories."

According to Webster, that's what we were in. Romantically, a thunderstorm is a kind of storm filled with excitement, beauty, and mystery, when viewed from the safety of one's bedroom window in the protection of one's home. Realistically, being in an electrical storm in the middle of the night, high on a ridgetop at approximately 1,100 feet above sea level, with no shelter except a few open Jeeps and trucks, was simply terrifying.

We didn't know what to do. Driving out was not an option. Neither was walking out. Our only real choice was to find whatever protection we could and wait for the morning light to come and, hopefully, the dissipation of the storm. Some found a modicum of safety and protection in the willow glen; it was damp, but a bit more sheltered. Others headed for the vehicles, either holding up inside or stretching out underneath them. This is where I retreated, finding a dry, relatively safe, but somewhat engine-scented bedding place. Needless to say, it was a restless night. Most of us counted the hours through the night, while counting the seconds between the lightning and thunder, hoping for a sign that the storm was departing. I imagined that most of the women were nicely warming themselves with the anger they felt toward my father for luring them to this change of pace and ambiance, camping!

As always, morning light did eventually come, The storm lessened and the rain stopped, at least for the time being. As on many mornings in the backcountry of the ranch, a type of fog settled in like a thick, wet, white blanket, enveloping the ridgetops. At such times, if there was any breeze at all, the moist white air moved about, shape-shifting, manifesting eerie

phantom-like figures swirling about. Visibility varied from minimal to extensive, depending on the thickness of the moisture.
On this particular morning, visibility varied quite drastically by
the moment.

At a relatively clear moment, the hunters among us decided
to wander out and try their luck, hoping to salvage the day. Others began gathering their gear and assessing the options of how
to get back to shelter. I decided to hunt, and proceeded eastward
and upward to an even higher elevation. I really had no reason
for choosing this direction except that others had gone a different way. It was not a good choice, at least as far as the hunting
went. The mist became progressively thicker the higher I wandered. I was unable to see anything but the trail and the brush
a few feet in front of me. But something inside me called me to
continue the adventure. It was a wet and weird scene. Moisture
dripped off the black gun barrel. White shadowy figures drifted
in and out of the sage on either side of the narrow dirt road.
I kept climbing toward a northeast viewpoint that would over-
look Lompoc, the Santa Ynez Valley, and Gaviota Pass. I knew
from other hunts that this vista was just ahead at the top of the
ridge. I'm not sure whether I intuitively knew that the mist might
clear if I could get to that place, but, like some gesture of divine
magic, as I approached the last few yards, I suddenly emerged
out of the thick, wet, white haze with a perfectly clear view to
the north.

This was the only time I ever had such an experience, other
than while flying in an airplane. From the top of the ridge, I
looked down over a sea of white, a solid layer of fog that covered
the entire panorama, excluding peaks that were as high as or
higher than me. These peaks emerged out of the thick white
cover like islands. It was a spectacular sight, like being on top
of the world. But although it was clear above the fog layer to
the north, when I turned and looked back toward the coast, the

fog was rolling heavily over the top of the ridge, like tiger claws scraping at the ridgetop.

The thunderstorm was clearly coming from the ocean side. It had pushed right up against the ridge and nestled itself against the mountains. I stood at the boundary between thunderstorm and inland fog bank, on the very line where one weather pattern stopped and another began. The energy caused by this weather mix was exhilarating. Chills of excitement shook my body, along with chills from the wet wind that was dampening my clothes. I stayed there as long as I could see, probably about a half-hour, living betwixt and between two weather systems. Then, suddenly, the thunderclouds began to swallow me up. The storm was returning; the crackling claps of thunder began again. As I stood on what seemed like uppermost pinnacle of God's earth with my .30–30 Winchester rifle in hand, I realized that I was now a human lightning rod. The precariousness of my situation suddenly hit me and, quite panicked, I immediately turned back into the storm and began to jog back down the hill toward the camp site, my heart pounding in my chest. The road down the hill seemed interminable, but the adrenalin was flowing and I hurried on, now fully aware of the danger.

When I reached the camp site, quite relieved, the hunters had returned and everyone was wondering where I had been. As I excitedly told them what I had seen, there were some very specific questions about my sanity, shaking of heads, and immediate retreating from my presence. It was clear that we needed to start the trek back, because the storm had resumed in earnest, and conditions were getting worse and worse. The thunder and lightning were becoming significantly more intense.

The muddy road was now impassible to vehicles, so we were forced to walk to the Hotel. Though the walk was truly miserable, with the constant danger of lightning and ankle-deep, sticky clay mud, I felt happy and somehow impervious. I had an odd sense that I had been blessed by a very special experience back there on the ridge, and that made the current misery seem insignificant.

We all made it back to the Hotel safely. The Jeeps and trucks were retrieved days later. There were no more camping trips planned by my father—nor by anybody else, for that matter. For the others, the memory of this event was probably not a pleasant one. But to me it was one of those episodes in the ranch wilderness, that would remain in my mind's eye forever, as if it were yesterday. I had been given a gift, a dangerous gift, but a gift of a special perspective on the natural world that I would probably never experience again. And, indeed, I never have.

To Know the Dark

To go in the dark with a light is to know the light.
To know the dark, go dark. Go without sight
and find that dark, too, blooms and sings,
and is travelled by dark feet and dark wings.

—Wendell Berry, "To Know the Dark,"
in *Farming: A Hand Book*

MY RECOLLECTIONS OF DARKNESS experienced at the
ranch always begin with a life-changing moment during an evening hunt in the summer of my twelfth year. Evening hunts were
almost daily occurrences during deer season, August and Sep-
tember. They involved the majority of the men at the ranch, as
well as boys who were old enough and who had some training
and experience in handling high-powered rifles. My brother and
I were included in these hunts from a very early age, about nine
years old.

This particular hunt was to focus on the east and west forks
of Bulito Canyon. If the hunt involved walking, we would usually
be dropped off by Jeep at the very back of a canyon or draw, or
on a ridgetop, and we would hunt down the canyon toward the
main road or the flatlands below, where the Jeep would collect
us and bring us home. I was walking up the west fork of Bulito
Canyon, which was different from the typical pattern in that the
canyon was deep and ran from east to west in the wildest part

of our ranch wilderness. It was a difficult hunt, for the walking was directly into the setting sun, but the wind was often down-canyon, which favored hunting up canyon. It was a beautiful canyon, trimmed at the top of the ridge with manzanita and tanbark oak groves that sloped down into open areas of sage and softer brush, great deer habitat.

I was to walk west up the canyon, hunting until sunset, turn around and walk back to the fork of the canyon to meet the Jeep where I had been dropped off. Along with others, who had been hunting the east end of the canyon, we would then drive home. Routine. Well, things didn't quite happen as planned. I went farther and slower up the canyon, losing myself, as I often did, in the magic of the hunt and the pure beauty of the elements sur-rounding me. I simply got caught up, mesmerized by the process and place. As it happened, it was quite dark before I realized that it was really quite dark and decided to turn around and hustle back. Since I was out quite far, walking back to the rendezvous point took longer than I expected. Accurate and appropriate thinking were clearly missing in this adventure. When I got back to where I was to picked up, it was not quite dark anymore. It was, as the phrase goes, "pitch black," which means dark as the darkest road, flat black darkness everywhere, no light, none at all.

The Jeep was not there. I waited awhile, but still it did not come. Fear began to creep into my body, all twelve years of it. I started to feel insecure, which translates into not being in a secure place, internally or externally, both of which were very true. I was more than three miles from home as the crow flies, and the crow was beginning to look more like a turkey vulture. I was in the back of the backcountry, where the wildest of the wild animals roamed. There was no moon, but I was deep in the canyon where the moon would have been hidden anyway. The steep canyon walls on the right and left made everything that much darker. The wind began to rustle the oak leaves, making an intermittent but ever-increasing hiss. My imagination began to hear things, big things. I thought about another hunting rendezvous with one of the older men that had gone awry. As he walked down a canyon through the brush in the dark, a wild boar charged up the trail. They collided in the dark. The man suffered a deep gash in his leg, never having seen the boar.

But this recollection wasn't helping me, so I changed my thoughts. I had a gun, a solid .30–30 rifle, the kind they used in the westerns on T.V. I was safe. Well, upon a second's further reflection, it occurred to me that you can't shoot what you can't see, and I couldn't see anything. More fear entered by body.

As I waited to be rescued, it became clear that something was not right. It was well past sunset, about nine o'clock at night. I needed to do something. I began to envision what I thought might be the best way home. There were two routes that I could see in my mind's eye. One of them, the winding road down the canyon and over a large ridge, would be very long. The other would be much shorter, straight down the canyon, not on a road but on a winding trail following the creek. I felt a degree of urgency, so I chose the shorter, quicker route and began walking through the black of night, deep in the canyon, the wind whistling, oak trees hissing, imagination aflame. But I was in motion. I was acting.

The darkness was simply terrifying at first. I moved slowly, struggling to see my next step. Though at first I was on the road, when I came to where the road left the creek line, I took the creek's path, the path less traveled, and as Robert Frost poetically posed, "and that made all the difference." Each step now was not only into pure darkness, but I could no longer predict where my foot would come down on the meager cow trail I was on. The whole process became a movement into the dark unknown.

I began to think I had made the wrong decision in choosing the trail rather than the road, but I had come too far to turn back now.

As I walked, straining to see my next step, I slowly began to notice that if, instead of forcing my sight into the darkness straining to see the trail, I relaxed my eyes and looked at the periphery of my visual field, I could actually see the trail better. I was fascinated by this.

Immersed in this process, I became progressively more comfortable in the darkness, excited by the realization that the less I *tried* to see, the less I looked for light to show me the way, the more I actually *could* see and the lighter the way seemed to be. I was soon moving quite rapidly along the trail, quite oblivious to the darkness. I was enjoying the movement, feeling my heart beat with excitement, as I walked through the wind and the rustling of the oak leaves. I was surprised that I did not feel afraid. I felt engaged and attuned to the dark wildness around me.

I now felt confident that my different way of seeing in the dark would keep me safe—safe enough to survive, that is. Yes, there were aspects of this wilderness that were threatening, but I would be fine. I would see my way back home in this night, and I did. The deep, dark, oak-filled canyon opened up to the low, rolling, dried mustard-stemmed landscape, the section of the ranch between the wild backcountry and the more domesticated flatlands below. The wind relaxed in the open space, like the water in a narrow river calms and quiets itself when it approaches the sea. I was practically home now that I was through the darkness of the oaks and the creek bed, or so it seemed. But I still had a good distance to walk.

When I finally walked into the house it was close to ten o'clock. I remember how warm the house was, almost too warm. I could feel my skin warming, almost stinging as it warmed from the night's cold air to the hot air in the kitchen. The air of domesticity and safety felt thick and stuffy. In a very specific way, I felt somewhat sad that my adventure was over, a surprising nuance of regret that I was now inside the house. When my parents asked what had happened, I found myself irritated by their concern. Why all the fuss? I was fine. I was great. In fact, I felt transformed. I felt older, more mature, and more confident deep down inside myself. Something had shifted in my relationship to myself. It was as if my feet were attached to the earth by a greater force of gravity. I simply felt more grounded within myself and in relationship to the world.

That night, and other night walks after, helped me become truly comfortable with darkness. Darkness was no longer something to be afraid of. It was something to experience and experiment with a different way of seeing. It became a place to practice seeing by not trying to see, to let go of the tendency to force focus and to unfocus into the darkness. This would prove to be an invaluable lesson that would assist me for the rest of my life, both personally and professionally as a psychologist. Stay with the darkness, look into it with soft eyes, and you will see things differently. The trail will appear.

Cowboys and the Roundup

The greatest beauty is
Organic wholeness, the wholeness of life and things,
The divine beauty of the universe.
Love that, not man
Apart from that...

—Robinson Jeffers, "The Answer,"
in *Such Counsels You Gave*
to Me and Other Poems

THE RANCH HANDS AND COWBOYS lived in a cluster of houses that were apart from most of the houses where the family lived. There was the usual implicit boundary between employers and the employed. And, as one might expect, there were cultural boundaries in that the majority of ranch hands were Hispanic.

From a child's perspective, there was the known world of the family, perhaps more honestly the somewhat known world of family, and the unknown world of the workers. For me, the world of the ranch workers was a world of mystery and intrigue, mainly because there were cowboys and horses over there. From about eight to twelve, I was particularly obsessed with cowboys. I wanted to be one! So I mustered up some courage and ventured into the cowboy world on the ranch, primarily on my own.

I still have a vivid image of setting my alarm, getting up at five in the morning all by myself and walking out of the house

into the early morning darkness and cool, damp air and directing myself up the long hill from our house to the horse saddling
barn. The hill to the barn was not steep or lengthy. But going
by myself and anticipating what might happen once I entered
the unknown world of the cowboys made it seem a long walk
filled with scary and ambivalent expectations. The road itself
was made of dirt and shale and had very tall old eucalyptus trees
lining both sides to protect the more domestic domain from
wind. These tall, straight trees were perfect perches for the
barn owl, screech owl, or great horned owl, and often on these
mornings the canyon would echo their screeches and hoots with
a blood-chilling resonance. The hooting, actually, was not so
nerve-wracking. There was, in fact, a degree of companionship in
it, and it was fun to try to establish communication with the owls
by returning their hoots. But the screech owls were different.
They would swoop down out of the trees in front of me, white-
feathered phantoms releasing the sound they are named for.
The screech would send my heart pounding and my adrenaline
rocketing out to the dark, star-riddled sky above. The positive
consequence of this early morning initiation was the immediate
warming up of my body, and an inner comfort that prepared
me for whatever was to come at the barn and beyond. I was so
apprehensive as I approached the barn that nothing much else
could have scared me to that degree. It was a long and challeng-
ing walk to that barnyard.

But I always managed to arrive at the horse barn, despite
these otherworldly experiences on my way up the hill. Once I
was at the barn another mysterious process began. I never knew
who would be there, not that I knew the cowboys well enough to
make it an emotionally secure place anyway. The dominant trait
of cowboys before sunrise is that they do not talk. They don't ever
talk much, but they are absolutely silent in the morning. They
move like shadows as they halter the horses, lead them into the

saddle barn, carry the saddles, blankets, and bridles from the tack room, and saddle the horses, all in the dark or dimmest of light, in complete silence. There is, of course, an occasional grunt, or more often an emanation of profanity or gas, but other than that it's a quiet world.

Being age eleven or so, and of uncertain mind, I usually needed some help somewhere in the saddling routine but not everybody was available. Some of the cowboys were quite actively unavailable, withdrawn into themselves, disgruntled in their sometimes hungover state, or merely struggling with the tough lives they were living. The ones who were lower down in the hierarchy didn't make much money and were there because they didn't have much else and needed to hide from more mainstream life. Though these cowboys would occasionally nod or wink, it didn't feel safe for me to engage with them.

However, there was another kind of cowboy whose manner was distinctly different. Even as a young boy, it was clear to me that some of these men were unique. They exuded absolute confidence, a firmness in all mannerisms, as they performed their tasks. It showed in the way they walked through the silence. They moved with an aura of certainty. Their posture was entirely natural, and their motions were precise. These were the men I instinctively looked to for help, and in fact they were the ones who were available to help me. They were the ones who loved what they were doing and welcomed the ranch owner's son's interest in their world. They wanted to show me their way, and took obvious pride in doing so. They were the true ranch hand elders to me, the ones closest to the earth. They were the real cowboys, the real horsemen. I wanted to be like them.

The head of the ranch hands was a man named Frank Pacheco. He was at the top of the hierarchy, the head horseman. It was primarily Frank who assisted me with saddling. To me he was the king of the cowboy world. I still remember a lesson he gave me in the nature of horses. Horses, he said, are much like people in that some really don't want to go to work in the morning. He said this as he grabbed a cinch, the leather belt that goes around a horse's belly and holds the saddle on. He proceeded to firmly knee the horse's underside, causing the animal to exhale, and quickly tightened the cinch, then buckled it tightly on the horse's belly. The horse gave us both a look of irritation. I immediately felt sorry for him. Noticing my concern, Frank smiled slightly and asked me, "Would you rather fall off this horse at a full gallop, or ride upside down?" The answer was obvious. He then explained how some horses, like some men, had ways of protesting the workday, and one way a horse protests was to fill himself with air while being saddled, then relax, loosening the cinch, making the saddle more comfortable and, if he was lucky, dispensing with the rider completely. It always struck me how well Frank seemed to know the inner world of horses, and how he would compare the nature and ways of horses with the nature and ways of his workers. I felt safe with Frank.

Once the horses were saddled, we mounted and began the slow ride out of the barnyard into the predawn darkness, heading toward the canyon that was the focus of the morning's roundup. There was essentially no talking at this point, merely the sound of horses breathing and snorting their displeasure, and the jingle of bridles mixed with the squeaking of the saddles, all grounded by the sound of hooves on the hard shale road. Now that I was astride my quarter horse, Tico, adjusting my saddle, reins, and body to the two thousand pounds of pure animal energy moving between my legs, I was a cowboy. I was a "man among men," and the experience was exhilarating. It was such a powerfully centering feeling. It was as if there were a tree trunk that entered the top of my head, went straight through the center of my body, branched out down my legs, ran out my seat and down through the horse, straight into the earth. This sensation of complete grounding was being stored in the deepest part of my physical, emotional, and future spiritual self, fortifying me. I felt godly atop that horse.

But there was more to come. Though there were many interesting occurrences on these roundups, the one that is particularly significant lies in the interaction of cowboy, horse, cow, and terrain. The interaction of these four in the wilderness can result in anything from complete chaos to something like a symphony. All four are intimately related, as is always the case in a wilderness ecosystem. The horses, cows, and environment would probably find their symphonic pattern on their own; man is usually the one who disrupts the rhythm.

Being a boy, I was often the problem. It was on these roundups that I first understood the proverb "There is nothing worse than a scared rider on a scared horse." A horse is like any animal. If, out of one's own anxiety, one attempts to impose one's will on the horse by pure force, the result is an escalation of anxiety. The horse becomes more agitated, and the rider begins to lose control. The cattle pick up on this and become distracted; they act out and may stray up draws or onto trails that run contrary to the landscape. This happened to me frequently because I was not sensitive to the instincts of the animal I was riding. Good cow ponies have good instincts. If the rider can give up trying to manage the horse and go with the instinct of the horse, the horse will herd the cows quite naturally, and the cows will accept being herded and follow the contours of the landscape. The symphony of man, horse, cow, and canyon plays out beautifully. But it all starts with man—in this case, me—relaxing into an instinctive relationship with the horse. The horse responds to that relaxed confidence, following his own instincts and reading the instincts of the cows and the canyon trails.

When at age ten or so I finally began to understand that I needed to let go of fear and the urge to control, the cowboy world became a different place. Everything on our rides seemed to merge into a kind of euphoric blur. Time seemed to disappear. There was a dream-like quality to these experiences. In fact, sometimes the combination of early rising, hunger, sun, and heat along with the easy interplay of all four players put me into a dreamy quasi-sleep. No, not asleep at the wheel, but in a way half asleep. Nevertheless, I was still relatively safe, aside from the occasional faltering of the horse's stride or the stronger but infrequent jolt as the horse reacted to a rattlesnake on or beside the trail. Mostly, though, I was lost in the mesmerizing trance of the roundup's interplay of man, horse, cow, and canyon that I was a part of, a very grounded part of a greater whole.

At the end of the roundup we returned to the barn. After several hours of riding we were hot, thirsty, hungry, and tired. We dismounted, unsaddled, wiped the horses down, and turned them out into the field. I vividly recall the moment my young feet hit the ground as I dismounted Tico. I felt as if I were about a foot tall, and that my legs would be stuck in a bowed curve for the rest of my life. It was very awkward to walk around as I gradually adjusted to the ground. Usually Frank helped me with much of this, as horses were tall and saddles were heavy. But my main feeling at this point was that I was one of them. I was a cowboy and had just finished a roundup.

Once everything was done I would start my walk, bow-legged as I was, down the hill from the barn to our house. I didn't feel like the same kid who had walked up the hill that morning. Something was different about me. I felt I had really been somewhere, accomplished something, and become somebody else. I felt older, more mature—simply put, more of a man. Though I didn't realize it then, more bricks had been laid on the platform of my masculine evolution. And, most importantly, as I entered the house with the family around, I no longer felt like a boy. As my boots hit the hard wooden floor, spurs a-jangling, I was, yes, a cowboy.

The Black Brant
and the Pacifico

Every region has its wilderness. There is the fire in the kitchen, and there is the place less traveled. In most settled regions there used to be some combination of prime agricultural land, orchard and vine land, rough pasture, woodlot, forest, and desert or mountain "waste." The de facto wilderness was the extreme backcountry of all that. The parts less visited are where the bears are. The wilderness is in walking distance—it may be three days or it may be ten. It is the far rough high end, or the deep forest swamp end, of the territory where most of you live and work. People will go there for mountain herbs, for the trap line, or for solitude. They live between the poles of home and their own wild places.

—Gary Snyder, *The Practice of the Wild*

I HAVE ALWAYS LOVED Gary Snyder's description of wilderness. It captures an essential truth about nature. Nature is not just nature; nature is varied and has in its variety qualities, or personalities if you will, unique to specific regions. The ranch was always the ranch in that it was this chunk of land located west of Gaviota, all of it wilderness compared to the nearby city of Santa Barbara; but the ranch had different regions within it, different poles, which had distinct qualities. Even on the ranch there was "fire in the kitchen" as well as areas less visited "where the bears are."

63

On the ranch, like anywhere else, we had our routines. There were places we frequented more than others, and there were places we rarely visited at all, usually because they were the "high rough end." Accessing those remote regions involved many things: driving farther in our Jeeps, walking farther, waking up earlier, taking more risks whether driving or walking. Just getting to these remote wild places always involved spending more time and energy. When we did venture to these places, however, they were, quite simply, distinctly different.

One of those more wild regions was Cojo Canyon. It was the last canyon on the Hollister Ranch and was the boundary between our ranch and the Bixby family ranch, called Cojo Ranch. More importantly, it was the last canyon before Point Conception, which is the point where the Pacific coast makes a ninety-degree bend from east-west to north-south. Whenever there is a place where one environment switches to another, as where the ocean meets the land, there is a boundary area, a betwixt and between, a transitional zone, which manifests a swirl of diverse energy. Cojo Canyon was just such a place, a transition zone for many things. And it was wild, very wild. It was far from "the fire in the kitchen."

For a child, venturing up the coast to the rather large bay at the mouth of Cojo Canyon was always an exciting journey. Usually I went there alone. I think it had to do with wanting to be alone in my own wildness. A specific mood would motivate me—rather, compel me—to this wild place. It was a long walk from the main house to Cojo Canyon. After a few canyons and their respective coves and points, the shoreline straightened out and was an easy walk. Walking steadily all alone always resulted in a kind of altered state, a trance, in which time seemed to disappear, my consciousness altered by the mesmerizing sound of ocean waves breaking and the progressive immersion in my solitude.

The spell would be broken suddenly when Cojo Bay came into view. The half-moon curve of the shoreline, cupping the blue-green bay, was distinct to the eye. Awakening to the feeling of this place was always memorable. It felt and looked mysteriously different. The waves broke large and long, rolling eventually onto the beach; the seaweed lying on the sand seemed to be more plentiful and more pungent; the sand was frequently carried away by the strong surf, leaving sand cliffs three or four feet high at the high tide line. And then there was the slough where Cojo Creek emptied into the sea. The combination of these features made Cojo Bay unique and seemingly more rugged than any other.

One of my strongest memories of Cojo Bay is the thrill of encountering a bird that I never saw anywhere else on the ranch. This was the black brant. I saw it on nearly every visit. In my childish imagination this bird was magical. I'm not sure exactly why it impressed me so; there isn't anything very spectacular about the bird. But it was interesting that I always saw this bird at Cojo, and nowhere else on the ranch. The black brant is not a duck; it's a goose. There were many ducks on the ranch, in the sloughs and reservoirs, but there were never any geese except at Cojo. For some reason, the brant seemed to instinctively and consistently choose that particular place on the ranch to set down. Its presence enhanced the mystique of Cojo Bay, and the bay enhanced the significance of the goose. Their association made this place an especially intense wilderness area.

The wilder any animal is, the more difficult it is to approach. When I saw a brant in the distance, usually on the periphery of the slough, I would crawl along the lower beach or tuck myself behind the tideline sand berms, moving slowly toward it. Most of the time I failed to get very close, as the birds had keen eyes, and were alert to the unusual. It was always disappointing not to get close enough to really see them. Occasionally, however, I could get close enough to really see the beauty of this bird: its night-black head, juxtaposed with the bright moon-white markings on either side of its neck that matched the markings on its tail and breast, made the brant a beautiful bird to behold.

These geese came from a long distance away, a land far off in my child's mind. I saw them only during the winter months, for they spent the breeding season in Canada. Only the winter migration brought the brants down to California. As a child I did not know where the geese came from. I only knew that they were not from here, that they had flown long way, and that of all the places on the ranch that they could land and rest, they chose only Cojo Bay. This made perfect sense to me. If I were a black brant, I would choose to rest in solitude at Cojo Bay as well. After all, as a child seeking adventure, when I wanted to settle into my solitude and my wildness, the wild and inspiring quality of this bay in particular made it the first place I would choose.

But Cojo Bay was not the only wild place that drew my attention. Cojo Canyon was a long and winding canyon with a substantial bend in the middle of its ascent to the ridgetop. The Spanish word *cojo* means "crooked-legged" or "lame." The name suits the canyon, for the course of the creek is bent or broken, deformed from the usual linear course. Starting on the beach at the slough, the creek winds around and eventually terminates in a box canyon high up on the northwest corner of the ranch.

The roads that converge on the top of the ridge are called De la Cresta and Cementario. De la Cresta, meaning "of the crest," is an appropriate name in that this road traverses the highest, roughest end of the ranch. From this ridgetop one can see the Channel Islands off to the southwest, as well as Jalama, Lompoc, and Gaviota Peak to the north and northeast.

Cementario meaning "cemetery," is the name of the upper-most end of Cojo Canyon road. I believe the name originated in Chumash mythology, in that an imaginary line extended from

Cojo Canyon to Point Conception, which was regarded as the gateway from the physical world to the spirit world to which, after death, souls traveled to the next life. Once again, Cojo marked a boundary, in this case between the physical world and the spiritual world, mythologically.

To get to the Cojo ridgetop was extremely difficult, even dangerous in places, especially if the dirt road had not been attended to for some time, which was typically the case since it was so far away and hard to get to. If the name Cementario did not originate from Chumash lore, the road might have been named for the sheer cliffs on the down-canyon side. Driving off the road even slightly here would almost certainly deliver a person to the *cementario*.

The road was treacherous to drive, and the walk was long and steep. Why, then, would we youngsters venture into this high, rough area? For one thing, it was always exciting to adventure there. It was, literally, "where the bears are"—as well as mountain lions. Even more alluringly, it was where a certain breed of deer lived, a deer we called the "Pacifico."

Most of the deer on the ranch were blacktail deer and the smaller California mule deer. They were found everywhere. The Pacifico, however, could only be found in the wildest parts of the ranch. If it could be found at all, for it really was scarce, it would be found only in the most rugged terrain of the backcountry, concealed during the day among the chaparral and tanbark oaks.

What was unique about this deer was its breeding. It was a cross between a blacktail deer and a mule deer. Like the black brant, the larger mule deer was an animal from lands far away—Montana, Wyoming, Idaho, high in the Sierra Nevada, northern California places more remote and wilder than the ranch. But somehow a hybrid of the "muley" had found its way to this coast, and in very few numbers resided there.

The Pacifico deer looked like where it lived: rough. It was a significantly larger and heavier deer than the blacktail. The antlers looked more like manzanita branches: thick, jagged, and prone to greater width and height. Its head was wide and snub-nosed, with mule shaped ears, its coloring a blend of rich dark brown, black, and silver-gray, its fur long, almost hairy in places. It was a wild-looking animal, almost disheveled in appearance.

To have any chance of finding this deer, we had to reach the area where it was mostly found before sunrise, so as to be there at sunrise. This meant leaving the hearth in the early morning darkness, manning our Jeeps, and journeying via the most difficult terrain to the most remote part of the ranch. The travel was long and often went through thick, damp, coastal fog, which impaired visibility on the old, narrow, and usually eroding road. But this is what we had to do if we were to arrive early enough to surprise these deer before they moved back into the tanbark oak shadows for protection from the oncoming day's heat.

The ridge where these deer could be found was just past the convergence of De la Cresta and Cementario roads, the upper end of the Cojo Canyon and the beginning of the Chumash entrance into the spirit world. This ridge was a boundary, a place of transition in every way, and if one quieted oneself and paid attention to this environment, a truly special quality of place could be experienced. To a young boy, it was exciting to be there; it seemed almost as if the place had an electrical charge to it; I felt completely alive to my senses, goose-bump exhilaration.

When, on some perfect day, we put binoculars to our eyes at first light and saw one or more Pacifico deer grazing and warming themselves below the line of tanbark oaks, it gave us an adrenaline thrill and a vision of true beauty. As the early morning sun caught the silver-gray fur and the deep, rich earth-brown of their magnificent antlers, all set against a backdrop of lush green chaparral, the collage of brilliant colors was moving. There is nothing more beautiful than the rising or setting sun shining on anything, but the combination of these specific wild entities, all together, enchanted by the early morning golden sunlight, was spectacular.

The memory of those moments is indelibly imprinted on me. The images are still crystal clear in my mind's eye, and I can still feel the exhilaration in my older soul today. As I write these lines, it is all with me, unusually so. I have a clear sense, that as a young boy and young man I was never more alive than during these remote ranch experiences at Cojo Bay and the Cojo ridgetop. If I were to put more fanciful terms to these wilderness encounters, I would call them magical, perhaps sacred, most certainly filled with the reverential power of the truly wild.

My imagination tells me that the wild nature of both the black brant and the Pacifico deer were instinctively drawn to and resonated with the wild energy of their respective wilderness domains. That is why they chose Cojo Bay and the Cojo backcountry. The bird and the deer both had primitive nature to them, as did those parts of the ranch. And those animals and those places were the perfect calling for the more wild part of my youthful nature, or so it seems.

Rubbernecking

Deer foot down scree
Picasso's fawn, Issa's fawn
Deer on the autumn mountain
Howling like a wise man
Stiff springy jumps down the snowfields
Head held back, forefeet out,
Balls tight in a tough hair sack
Keeping the human soul from care
On the autumn mountain
Standing in late sun, ear flick
Tail flick, gold mist of flies
Whirling from nostril to eyes.

—Gary Snyder, "This Poem Is for Deer
(Hunting 8)," in *Myths and Texts*

MY GRANDFATHER REFERRED TO hunting as "rubber-necking." Not prone to saying much at any time, he would simply say, "I think I'll go rubberneck around." According to the family mythology, what that meant essentially was that the family needed some venison, and he was going to go get it. He was going deer hunting. It was said that he always knew where the deer were, so it is my assumption that he would hunt a particular area, knowing that a deer lived there, and "rubberneck" around until he was successful in finding food for the family.

My aunt Jane told me a story that she carried throughout her life. She was quite young, about eight, and had had some involvement with low-caliber firearms. Her brothers had more experience, but not much more, for all children were treated essentially the same, male or female. Her introduction to hunting occurred when the Chinese cook handed her a gun and said in broken English, "Here, it's time you help with cooking. Go get dinner." So off she went to rubberneck around for dinner.

By the time my generation was of hunting age, which started about age seven or eight, hunting for dinner had become a combination of food for family and recreation. My father had one absolute rule that all the children had to adhere to, and this rule was his attempt to address the importance of constructive hunting as compared to destructive hunting, and it was even more important when recreational hunting became part of ranch life. My father's rule was: "Whatever you shoot, you eat." He was absolutely rigid in this philosophy, and although it seems simple, it entails a rather complicated approach to one of the oldest rituals in human history.

My father was not revered by the upper echelon of hunters on the ranch. When I was a child looking through the lens of the more "successful" hunters, those on top of the pecking order, I could see that my father's gun was too small, he didn't drive a large powerful truck, he mostly hunted on foot rather than driving, he didn't hunt frequently, and he never told stories about his conquests. He simply didn't seem to be the John Wayne type, which to my impressionable mind was the model to look up to. Nothing could have been further from the truth, however. Ego and power, machismo, had nothing to do with the essence of hunting, nothing to do with hunting magic, and nothing to do with the sacred ritual. It took me a while to figure this out.

My father hunted differently. He hunted with the smallest deer rifle used on the ranch, a .30–30 Winchester, and also with the largest and heaviest binoculars used by anyone on the ranch. He spent less time driving, more time walking and, especially, more time sitting than anyone else. While others were driving up and down canyons in their big trucks carrying high-powered rifles and covering as much territory as possible, my father would stay in one place, scanning the hillsides with his huge binoculars. Since my father's way of hunting was so different, and since my grandfather had taught my father to hunt, I have to surmise that when my father and I hunted together, we were rubbernecking around, hunting the old-fashioned way.

I can remember every hunt my father took me on. They were all very similar in process and result. However, one of them in particular holds all the wisdom of his way. Given that my father was a physician and worked long hours, it was a special occasion when he came to the ranch and asked me to hunt with him the next morning. He did so one evening when I was about thirteen. The plan was to drive up to the head of Bulito Canyon, the main canyon on the ranch, park the Jeep on the side of the road, and walk up what was referred to as the west fork of Bulito Canyon.

Following the usual routine, we rose before sunlight, ate something minimal, climbed into a Jeep open to the cold morning air, and set off up the canyon in silence. My father never talked much anyway, but on these morning hunts he was even more quiet. It was a crystal clear morning, with neither inland nor coastal fog. Visibility was perfect.

We arrived at the top of the canyon, up against the last ridge at the back of the ranch, and parked the Jeep. Firearms and binoculars in hand, we began to walk up the west fork. We were walking west, with the rising sun behind us illuminating the hillsides in front of us, which was ideal. Early morning sun imparts its own kind of radiance. The wind, though minimal, was moving down the canyon from west to east. Wind direction was crucial, for if it were blowing east to west, the deer would smell us long before we had a chance to see them. The fork of this canyon began among oak trees, and, wanting to reach location where we would have better visibility, we walked somewhat quickly through the trees. It was absolutely silent except for the crisp crunching of dried leaves on the ground and the soft rustling of the morning breeze moving through the oak branches all around us.

It was an exhilarating morning's beginning for me, filled with anticipation and excitement. I was with my father, which was special in itself, the day was beautiful in the conditions it provided us, and we were hunting. It is difficult to explain to people who have never been on a hunt what the experience is. In evolutionary terms, not much time has elapsed since humankind needed to hunt in order to survive. The primal hunt is still psychologically accessible within us. Being on a hunt means being completely immersed in nature, seeing, feeling, hearing, and smelling with heightened acuity, all senses alert. This is the way a hunter has to be in order to meet the animal on its own level.

In my youthfulness, excitement would get the best of me, and I would begin to hurry. I did so this morning, and the first words I heard from my father were, "Slow down, don't force it." These words meant I was to hunt my dad's way, which isn't easy for an exuberant thirteen-year-old. Looking back as an adult, I see that these words meant get your ego out of the process, refrain from acting on the environment and let the environment act on you, be in pain with patience, open yourself to what is happening around you, relate to the animal you are hunting, and pay attention to your relationship to the physical world around you. Though this was difficult for me to understand as well as to do, I wanted to be a good son, so I tried hard to cooperate.

But the most painful part of the patience was yet to come. When we had walked through the oak trees for about forty-five minutes, treading carefully to avoid noise, the trees began to thin and the more open part of the canyon became visible. Now it was time to sit for an eternity, as it seemed, and use our binoculars to drift over the landscape lit by the golden rays of sunrise. Rather than move forward more aggressively, we would sit, stay quiet, and be patient. This was my father's hunting process, rubbernecking around with those big binoculars.

Able to see hundreds of yards with great detail, my father would often sight deer. In fact, I cannot remember when he did not. He did so this morning. Based on its size and the thickness of its antlers, the buck he sighted was an older deer. Having pointed out the deer to me and shown me how to stalk it by drawing a diagram in the dirt on the trail, my father told me to go on alone while he stayed behind to watch. His parting words to me were, "Pay attention and be patient." Then off I went, hunter and hunted merging into the ancient ritual.

The buck was about six hundred yards away and had not detected us. He was up the left side of the canyon, just below the line of tanbark oaks. The plan was to walk slowly up the bottom of the canyon along the trail, at all times keeping my eyes on the deer's movements, until I came to the small ridge just before the ridge the buck was on. Here I would climb the ridge, always careful to stay downwind, and hopefully surprise the buck at a distance of fifty to one hundred yards, good shooting range for my .30–30 Winchester. Though this may seem straightforward, it was not so at all.

Deer have senses. Their vision, sense of smell, and hearing are exceptional. They raise their heads frequently as they graze, putting their noses into the air as their ears rotate and their eyes glance side to side scanning the terrain. However, beyond their keen senses it has also seemed to me that they notice other things that make them become alert. I mostly notice this in the scrub jays. On this particular morning hunt, there seemed to be more jays about than usual. Whenever the jays noticed me, they would squawk and fly about. When they did this, the deer became suddenly very alert, stopping their grazing and looking intently about for longer periods of time than usual. There seemed to me to be another source of information that helped them detect danger. Whenever this happened, I had to completely stop and wait. The deer seemed to have been told explicitly that something alien was in the environment, which was true.

So I walked slowly and patiently, trying hard to adhere to my father's words. I stayed close to the upper side of the road, intermittently peering through the brush to check the movement of the deer, as I tried to read his reading of his world. When his head lifted, I froze; when it lowered, I moved. When the jays became flustered, I waited longer.

I eventually came to where I had to climb up the ridge to the line of tanbark oaks. I chose a slight groove in the hillside, a bit of a wind channel that kept my smell and sound moving away from the deer. I started up the slope, watching where my feet landed so as to not step on noisy leaves or twigs. But about half way up I noticed that the deer was moving away from me and would soon cross over the crest of the ridge that he was on. He did so, and disappeared. It was my intuition that the deer had sensed that something was amiss, and he was moving on toward the trees above for protection. I had to make an instinctive decision. I had to anticipate where he was going and move swiftly down then up the ravine separating us, hopefully coming over the ridge at a point where I would encounter him before he went into the trees. I went into action.

The brush at the bottom of the ravine was thick and wet. It took real effort to plow swiftly through it, and my clothes became wet and heavy. I then climbed up the far side of the ravine. Just before topping the ridge that the buck had been on, I stopped, wet, tired, and panting, to quiet myself, as my father had taught me to do. Rushing over a ridgetop when out of breath makes it impossible to aim a rifle accurately, should that be immediately required. Calmer now, I crawled quietly through the brush, crested the ridge slowly, and began to scan the other side. At first I saw nothing; it seemed my instincts had been off. Then, straight across the canyon from me, standing just below the line of trees, stood the buck, staring directly at me. It was a moment of mutual surprise. We were eye to eye, frozen in time. The deer could easily have moved into the dense trees just above him, but he didn't. The world seemed so still and quiet as the two of us just watched each other, both completely motionless, for what seemed like a long time. I slowly raised my gun, little by little. I aimed, took a deep breath, and shot. The hunt was over.

I climbed the hundred yards or so up the ridge to where the deer lay. He was much bigger than I thought. I felt very proud that I had been successful, so I turned around and shouted to my father down in the canyon, "I got him! He's a big one!" I heard my father shout back, "Yes, saw it all. I'll go get the Jeep." Now I felt even more elated because my dad had seen the whole hunt. This lasted about a minute, until I realized how much work I had to do. Since my father was going to get the Jeep, I was on my own to field-dress the deer and drag it down the ridge to the road—a very tough task that my father obviously wanted me to perform by myself. I did so with great effort, and my father met me in the Jeep shortly after I got the deer down to the road. He looked at the deer then looked at me, and said with a subtle smile, "Nice one. Good job. Let's get him into the Jeep."

We hefted the buck into the Jeep and drove off in silence. And that was all! I would have liked more praise from my father, and I felt a momentary hint of disappointment. But I soon realized there would be no more words about the hunt, nor need of them. I gradually understood that my father's slight grin had told me he was proud, and that was enough. Deep down, it was very satisfying to have rubbernecked around on the ranch with my father in another successful hunt, the old way.

HUNTING EPILOGUE

Though I felt that something unique had happened that day, that hunt and a few others like it would make more sense later on in my life. Referring to Native American hunting mythology, Joseph Campbell states that the hunting process and the relationship between hunter and hunted becomes a kind of agreement in which the animal is "a knowing participant in a covenanted sacred act." In "This Poem Is for Deer," Gary Snyder, in a similar vein poetizes,

> *Deer don't want to die for me*
> *I'll drink sea-water*
> *Sleep on the beach pebbles in the rain*
> *Until the deer come down to die*
> *in pity for my pain.*

As much as humans attempt to dissociate themselves from their animal origin, we are, irrefutably, in our primal depths, still animals. We are related to animals, and they are related to us; we are both part of the wild. Native Americans understood this relationship as well as how it played out in the ritual of hunting.

My father's way of hunting was closer to the old tradition than anything else around me when I grew up. It was a way to hunt that was highly respectful of the animal hunted and of the environment in which the hunting took place. It was a way of hunting and thinking that opened the door to another world, one that we humans do not inhabit much at all, a paranormal world in which there really is communication between humans and animals, animal to animal. Traditionally, hunters lived in a world in which the paranormal was a pervasive everyday phenomenon. The portal to this world is intuition and instinct. Animals live constantly in the world of intuition, instinct, environmental awareness, and extrasensory kinds of communication. To relate to animals, we humans need to access these latent abilities within us.

This is not meant to be a defense of hunting. It is a statement about the importance of relating intimately to wilderness and the animals that inhabit the wilderness. By doing so, we become aware of the instinctual world within us, a world which assists us in quite simply living a more vital life, as well as in understanding more deeply the importance of preserving the wild.

For me, relationship to the instinctual life and its possibilities came through the medium of hunting and the wisdom of the hunting ritual. I do not hunt with a gun anymore; I hunt with a camera. Although over the years I have become more benumbed to nature by my relationship with the civilized world than I was as a child on the ranch, I still have access to that paranormal otherworld when walking in the wilderness. It is always right there, as long as I can curtail my propensity to hurry and be quiet, still, and patient enough to listen to the intuitions and instincts within. Whenever I am able to enter the world of the wild, the animals appear, and memories of hunts with my father reemerge. At those times I feel genuinely blessed for having the opportunity to "rubberneck around" on the ranch with my dad.

The Last Dance

*When the imbecility, betrayals, and disappointments
    become apparent, what will you have, but to have
Admired beauty? I believe that the beauty and nothing
    else is what things are formed for. Certainly the world
Was not constructed for happiness nor love nor wisdom.
    No, nor for pain, hatred and folly. All these
Have their seasons; and in the long year they balance
    each other, they cancel out. But the beauty stands.*

—Robinson Jeffers, "Invasion"

IN 1961, JOHN J. HOLLISTER, my grandfather, the patriarch
and ranch consolidator, passed away. His death set off a period
of four years of intense family feuding over whether to sell or
maintain the ranch. In 1965 it was finally decided that the ranch
would be sold, and it was. Though the ranch would change ownership over the next five years, for those of us whose lives were
centered around the ranch, the one hundred years of family
ownership was over. We had to leave.

I remember the final day on the ranch as if it were yesterday,
but it was the spring of 1965. As I sit now at my desk in front of
the window, which looks out over Cojo Canyon where coastal
fog crawls up the draw, the images of that final day on the ranch
are vivid in my memory, and the heavy feeling lingers within it.

We were all gathered at "the Ritz," the ranch-style house

81

that had been the family's communal hearth for many years. There was a large contingency of adults and a substantial group of youth. Everyone who had frequented the ranch over the years was present, plus several guests.

From the beginning of the gathering, late in the day, just before dusk, there had been an atmosphere of a big party, a seemingly festive occasion; yet the air was tainted by another mood as well, one that could only be described as weirdness. Something was off, but my unsophisticated seventeen-year-old mind couldn't figure it out. It all just felt disorienting. The adults started to imbibe early, earlier than usual, while the younger group wandered around somewhat awkwardly. Eventually dinner was served, and everyone sat at the table and ate and continued to drink, as the energy in the house progressed toward chaotic social turbulence. After dinner the adults moved into the big living room, where the fire was ablaze. The drinking continued, and I remember myself and my peers realizing spontaneously and collectively, that we needed to go outside and get away from the awkward atmosphere inside. We unconsciously understood that we needed to have our own wake, in our own way.

So we all climbed into our Jeeps and cars and headed out into the night, sleeping bags and music tapes in hand, toward an unknown destination. The exhilaration of being out of the house and in the fresh cold air of the night was palpable. Riding in the open Jeeps—some in seats, some standing, some on the hoods—speeding through the darkness with two meager headlights illuminating only a few yards in front of us, the night air stinging our faces, we felt a sense of anarchic freedom. Just as the adults were having their intoxicated craziness in the house in their way, we had our own craziness outdoors in our way.

It was nighttime recreation to drive down the black oil-topped roads looking for kangaroo rats that liked to sit on the roads, which retained heat from the sun of the day. Once one was spotted, one, two or maybe three of us would try to catch it, a feat next to impossible, as these creatures were appropriately named. Most of the fun was watching the chase, friends making complete fools of themselves, running around ridiculously, disappearing over embankments and emerging again out of the darkness, scraped and bruised but laughing hysterically.

On this night we did the rat hunt to excess, burning off some of the weird anxiety we all experienced but did not understand. After a couple of hours roaming the night roads, we gathered to decide where to circle our wagons for the rest of the night. We settled on San Augustine Canyon, down deep in the draw amid a cluster of pepper trees close to a eucalyptus grove, good protection from the wind if needed. In spring at the ranch, the mustard plants grew thick and tall like grass, and sprinkled among the mustard stalks were horse thistles. Mustard was fairly innocuous, but horse thistle, despite the beauty of its purple flower, had sharp spikes surrounding the flower. Horses ate those buds, something I have never understood, because to human touch they were painful. We chose to camp in a pasture of mustard and horse thistles, only because it was somewhat covered, umbrella like, by pepper trees. This is where we would spend our last night on the ranch.

We parked the cars and Jeeps in a circle, then began to play music. My brother had a Willys Jeep completely rigged for great sound, as his vehicles always were. We turned the speakers around so they faced into the circle, put in a tape, and turned the volume up. There was some drinking and smoking, conversation and laughter, and attempts to find places to bed; but mostly we were drawn to the music inside the circle of cars, all surrounded by the darkness of the moonless night beyond. Nobody said a word about this being our last night on the ranch, but inside each of us, and certainly inside me, there was a subtle but deep pit in the stomach. Something was happening, and it was not good. And so the chaos escalated.

Jimi Hendrix, the Jefferson Airplane, the Eagles, Jackson Brown, the Beatles—the music kept flowing, the volume increasing. We built a small fire at the center of the circle and then it started to happen. The movement began as playful and silly, boy-girl, boy-boy, girl-girl, and then simply in one collective entity we began to dance, bumping, pushing, falling, and stomping our way through the mustard and thistle. Being a somewhat more reserved spirit, I watched it happen for a while before I, too, became part of the frenzy. I felt that there was some edge, some threshold that we were approaching, and that because of this excitement and fear we were about to go beyond that boundary. This was the sixties, and that edge was always near in some way. But there was something different and more intense about what was happening now. It was a final expression of the total freedom that ranch life had given us, mixed with bewilderment and unconscious anger over our impending loss. Whatever was rumbling around inside of us, we were acting it out in the extreme, and the dancing went on.

The party went on late into the night. The circle expanded as more of us joined the dance. Everyone seemed oblivious of the tall mustard and horse thistles. Occasionally someone would wander out into the pasture alone, into the mustard maze and the darkness of the night, only to reappear again and join in the central circle's cavort. Eventually, however, our energy began to wane, and then something quite interesting happened. As we slowed down, there was some eye contact and acknowledgement made subtly, then some arms were put to shoulders, and gradually we all formed a circle, arm-in-arm. Looking down at the earth and trampled weeds at our feet, occasionally looking up at each other, we stopped time for a moment in a symbolic and completely spontaneous declaration of companionship, all quietly honoring what this moment really meant. There were no words spoken, no need for words and moreover no ability to put this experience into words. We were too young for any eloquence of that kind. The moment, like the entire evening, was born and played out by pure instinct. The raw wisdom of impulsive instinct lead us all the way through that night.

Gradually the circle broke up, and a quieter kind of chaos began to take over. No one knew what to do next except to find a place to throw down a sleeping bag and drift off the sleep, for we were all quite thoroughly exhausted. I don't remember the night beyond that. I only remember the morning, the night being probably quite brief after our long revels.

When we awoke, we saw a scene of pure bedlam, an early morning of mayhem. Our first discovery was that we were not just among mustard and thistles, we were in a cow pasture, with an abundance of fecal remnants lingering around our camp site. One of us had even slept directly on top of one fairly fresh deposit. It was the polar opposite of the experience of the night before. Where there is an up, there is a down, and you can't get much further down than sleeping in cow dung. We were quite disoriented as we wandered around picking things up and observing the amazing terrain of last night's ceremony. One of our group had to leave more quickly, probably due to an overload of discomfort, and in backing out his vehicle he ran right over the ice chest, demolishing it. It was a perfect parting gesture and a fitting contribution to the morning's atmosphere.

And that was it. We eventually left the pepper tree grove behind and scattered into the future of that day and the future of our lives without the ranch. The ranch had been sold, we had our last dance, and most of us never returned. I have never spoken to anyone about that evening. In fact, most of us have never spoken at all about how losing the ranch affected us. I think it was too painful. Four generations of ownership had come to an end. It marked the end of an era, and the end of our youth. But even though the sadness of that day still lingers some fifty years later, we certainly went out in flames, and this last dance on the ranch, our farewell ritual, a combustion of pure spontaneity, instinct, and grief, will live inside me forever.

PART II

Reconnection

I only went out for a walk, and finally concluded to stay out till sundown. For going out, I found, was really going in.

—John Muir,
John of the Mountains: The Unpublished Journals of John Muir

Grief

One who remains passive when overwhelmed with grief,
loses the best chance of recovering elasticity of mind.

—Charles Darwin, *The Expression of the*
Emotions in Man and Animals

THE DAY I BEGAN my reconnection with the ranch is crystallized in my mind. Fifteen years after the ranch was sold, an old high school friend, who now owned a parcel of the ranch under the new owners' system, invited me out to the Santa Anita beach, my childhood power place, to have what he referred to as a "mussel bake." This was a foreign concept to me. When I was a child growing up on the ranch, we never even considered mussels as something to eat. Rattlesnakes, yes, but not mussels. It was a beautiful day blessed by a very low tide that revealed an abundant supply of mussels on the rocks and an occasional crab hiding under the mats of silky green eelgrass. It was the first time I had stepped onto ranch soil in the fifteen years since our last dance ritual evening.

The afternoon passed pleasantly enough, but I was in a detached, observing mode, almost sleepwalking through the mussel-gathering process. Then, as we were gathered around the big mussel-boiling pot, I noticed the sun approaching the horizon. I turned away from the others and walked off to the edge of the bluff to honor the beauty of the closing day.

I only went out for a walk, a short walk, but my saunter led me
to a point overlooking the slough, with the beach on one side
and the shale cliff promontory in the distance, and a view up the
canyon on the other side, all in the glow of the setting sun. The
vibrant golden sunrays of dusk radiantly lit up all of the natural
elements set before me: the rich tan of the dried mustard stalks
and summer grass, the white sand of the beach emerging from
the blue-green ocean in the distance, the dark green elephant
grass bordering the winding breeze-rippled slough, the silver-
gray driftwood scattered around the edges of the creek's outflow.
It was an evening scene that began to penetrate the storehouse
of my childhood memories. The beauty of this wilderness was
beginning to melt my unconscious denial and repression.

Then, as a pair of blue-winged teal circled in from over the
ocean, wings intermittently stationary as they glided in unison
through the evening air, webbed feet out as they set down on
the glassy slough, my emotions completely overtook me. Fifteen
years of unconscious grief burst out of me, a cathartic flash flood
of tears and memories. The emotions were a mixture of sadness,
anger, love, and excitement all at once. It was as if I had just been
reunited with a beloved long-lost friend, someone who had been
taken from my life abruptly and unjustly and who now stood
before me.

It was a brief moment in reality, but enormous subjective-
ly. Standing in the evening's beauty, emotions flowing forth, I
incredulously asked myself, "Doyle, how could you possible have
manipulated yourself into believing that what is before you right
now was not absolutely central to your life?" I was astonished
that I had managed to completely block out the meaning of this
personal landscape of my life for a decade and a half.

As the sun gradually slipped down behind the promontory, I
tried to compose myself so that I could reengage with the social
occasion. But as I walked back to the group it was clear that the

man walking back was a different man from the one who had walked innocently away to watch the sunset. I was now alive to the pain of the loss of this land, which, until that moment, I had thought I had moved on from, perhaps hadn't needed to experience at all, or just didn't leave. Now, ambushed by the beauty of my childhood's wilderness, I was alive to the depth of my connection to this special place in nature and in my soul. The outside and inside of me were now aligned, united by grief.

Although it was exhilarating to awaken to such a vital part of myself, I was now opened up to the true pain I had inside. Now, rather than a soul at peace, I was a soul more alive but more tormented. The anger boiled wildly inside me, mixed with sadness, despair, and longing. It was amazing to me that a piece of land could evoke such intense emotions, as powerful as the emotions called forth by the death of a family member, and even more so. It was a bewildering experience, but even more bewildering was my confusion over what I was to do with those emotions. In fact, the greater concern was what those feelings were going to do with me. A wilderness of grief had its claws in me in a powerful way, and I could do nothing but stay alive to it and let it point the way. A new journey was beginning.

On Being Lost

I talk to my inner lover, and I say, why such rush?
We sense that there is some sort of spirit that loves birds,
    animals and the ants—
Perhaps the same one who gave a radiance to you in your
    mother's womb.
Is it logical that you would be walking around entirely
    orphaned now?
The truth is you turned away yourself,
and decided to go into the dark alone.
Now you are tangled up in others, and have forgotten
    what you once knew,
and that's why everything you do has some weird failure
    in it.

—Kabir, "I Talk to My Inner Lover,"
in *Kabir: Try to Live to See This*

AFTER THE MUSSEL bake at Santa Anita beach, where after fifteen years of repression I became alive to my grief over the loss of the land, I realized how lost I really was. Relationships with people and things of intimate personal value define who we are and give us identity. When we lose those relationships, we lose part of our identity. In essence, we become lost. Being lost renders us ill at ease in an emotional, mental, and spiritual way. Inside the experience of unease, there exist many negative emotions: anxiety, panic, restlessness, confusion, dissociation, depression, alienation and, the ultimate demon, fear, which underlies all. Though for many people numbness seems preferable to the experience of unease, being awake to pain means being more alive to the world and one's self, as uncomfortable as that may be. There is also a far greater chance for personal evolution when one is alive to pain than when one is dead to it. But that is easier said than done.

Being alive to loss, grief, and the pain therein requires one to respond to the pain, if any personal evolution is to take place. To be responsive to pain and its source is to pursue healing, and healing can take a person on many interesting pilgrimages.

In pursuit of reconnecting myself to my ranch wilderness heritage, one pilgrimage took me to Wyoming in search of property that might be more affordable than California. My old childhood stomping grounds had become quite unaffordable. I became obsessed with the notion that Wyoming was the last frontier, and possessed by the belief that if I did not seek out and acquire some wilderness property now, right now, it would be too late, and becoming a landowner would be lost to me and my children forever. I was quite out of my mind, but that's what being lost is truly about.

I took ten days off from work, after convincing my wife that this journey was imperative (she knew I was crazy but respectfully and perceptively kept quiet), flew to Cheyenne, rented a car, and set out looking for my ranch. My ideal was a property that backed up to a national forest, so that I could wander in the wild endlessly! Unconsciously, it was an attempt to recreate what I had grown up with on the ranch: vast wilderness space and freedom.

From Cheyenne I journeyed to Saratoga, Pinedale, Dubois, Greybull, Sheridan, Newcastle, Wheatland, and back to Cheyenne, almost a circle at the center of the state. I drove about 1,500 miles. There were the wetlands, wide-open plains, the east and west sides of the Big Horn Mountains, and sometimes a combination of these, as in the town of Sheridan. I would contact realtors, look at properties, talk about land and dreams and history, and call home each night to say that, although I had seen some beautiful property, I hadn't yet found what I was looking for. It is quite obvious to me now that what I was looking for didn't really exist, and it certainly was not to be found in Wyoming, as amazingly beautiful as Wyoming was.

The absurdity of what I was doing came through to me quite suddenly. I had arrived in Greybull and met up with my cousin's friend, who owned and worked a small ranch high on the west side of the Big Horn Mountains. It was a beautiful place. The terrain around Greybull is very dry and desolate, at least in October, almost an ash gray moonscape. As I drove through that otherworldly terrain, I felt that I was not in my element. Then, like magic, as I came over a ridge, the landscape completely changed. I had crossed the snowfall line, and the lunar surface abruptly gave way to a rich green and heavily foliated world. And, almost immediately, there before me was my cousin's friend and his ranch.

Press was his name, and he lived in a beautiful stone house with a large reservoir in front that reflected the timber-lined mountain above, which was crossed by what Press referred to as the elk trail—true wilderness. This was a late spring, summer, and early fall Wyoming paradise, which, as Press quickly informed me, turned into an absolutely uninhabitable winter world, a cold and frozen hell. Press was a man who never stood still. From morning till night he was tending to the sheep, the cattle, the water, the horses, the house, the barn—ceaseless motion, all with a sense of urgency. Though I was essentially useless to him, not being particularly handy, I did what I could to assist him until I needed some quiet time to myself. I needed to wander alone.

Press suggested a hiking route, and I headed out early one morning. That morning was the most exhilarating part of my trip. This was a beautiful wilderness adjoining the national forest, which gave it a sense of infinite space and freedom. I was on my feet, walking alone, wandering in the wild, just like on the ranch. The view as I climbed gradually higher was magnificent, even with the moon-like terrain in sight far below. I discovered a creek and began to wander up it to see where it came from, thinking that perhaps it would take me directly to the crest of the mountains. Though I stayed with the creek for a good distance, it soon became clear that I could not ascend any farther without risk of harming myself. So I stopped, sat down beside the running water, and looked out over the Big Horn Mountains and the Greybull gray, taking in all of where I was.

There it came to me. I was by myself, nobody for miles, no family, no friends, a lone fourth-generation Californian, one Hollister up a creek again, but now in the middle of a Wyoming wilderness. True, I was enjoying the wilderness as wilderness; but now it became excruciatingly clear just how lost I really was. Although it was truly beautiful, this was not *my* wilderness home. The terrain was magnificent, but it didn't resonate with my personal experience of wilderness. I was still orphaned from my heritage, lost here in an alien Wyoming wild. Once again, that deep sense of sadness and despair entered my body.

Psychologically, Greybull Creek was the end of my pilgrimage in Wyoming, even though I continued to explore, always hoping for the right property to appear. But the final lesson of this journey only came to me when I was back at home—and I use the word "home" quite specifically. Having returned from Wyoming, I went back to work the next day at my job as a psychologist, back to shepherding my human flock. Finished for the day, I locked up and went out into the waning light of dusk, when suddenly a gust of wind shook the branches of the oak tree above my office. The early evening sunlight mixed with the breeze in the oak limbs above stopped me dead in my tracks. It became clear to me in that moment. *This* was my home. This California live oak, with the wind rushing through it, was my home. Wyoming, or any other wilderness away from the specific landscape I grew up in, would not, could not, be my personal wilderness home. Those other wildernesses could be wonderfully beautiful to me, and a home in the more general sense of an earth household, but they could not be *my* wilderness home on the deepest, most intimate personal level, home to my soul. I had to be *here*, where the live oak grows and the wind blows through it making that memorable, magical sound.

Something very important had happened in Wyoming. By immersing myself in sadness and *angst*, the unease from the loss of my landed heritage, I was forced to confront the need to retain my connection to wilderness. Wyoming was an important stage in the grieving process. Symbolically, it was a gesture to the realm of activity rather than passivity and depression. I was still utterly lost, still orphaned, but my understanding of what was ultimately meaningful had become clearer. Being connected to "my home" in wilderness meant being connected to a landscape like the one I'd grown up in. The California central coast landscape was my personal landscape and wilderness. Each of us has his or her personal wilderness home, one that is similar to that of our childhood, or that has a special connection to our soul. It is essential for each of us to maintain our connection to both our personal wilderness and to wilderness in general. If we do not, crucial psychological and spiritual experiences are lost. The wilderness of Wyoming, one of my human homes, had helped me define the importance of being connected to the more intimate personal wilderness of my childhood. My journey was not over, but its purpose and meaning were becoming clearer.

Return to Silence

God is the friend of silence. See how nature—trees,
Flowers, grass, grow in silence; see the stars, the moon
And the sun, how they move in silence.... We need silence to
Be able to touch souls.

—Mother Teresa, *A Gift of God*

WHEN THE RANCH WAS SOLD, there were two family elders
who had longtime intimate relationships to the most beautiful
part of the entire ranch. That part was referred to as the Santa
Anita Ranch, or originally, El Rancho de Nuestra Señora del
Refugio. The Santa Anita Ranch is where my father, Clinty, and
his fraternal twin, Jane, had grown up. It is also the part of the
ranch where I had grown up, and is still referred to as the Hollister Ranch. Clint and Jane took very different paths after the
ranch was sold. Though it is a very long and tortuous story, it suf-
fices for this occasion to say that my father was so overwhelmed
by the pain of the loss that he cut himself off from all connection
to it and did not take the option of buying a smaller portion back
when it was offered. This would have maintained my connection
to the land and my heritage. Need more be said?

My father's sister, Jane Hollister Wheelwright, chose a different road. When the ranch was sold, she climbed up onto
her horse, as she was wont to do, and spent weeks riding over
the entire Santa Anita Ranch, canyon by canyon, revisiting her

memories and allowing her emotional life to progress naturally, all the while keeping her journal. She addressed the closing of an era and began to envision how she would maintain her relationship with the land in a new and different way. The result was ownership of one hundred acres in the remote northwestern corner of the old ranch, at the head of the last canyon, Cojo Canyon. There she retired with her husband, Jo. In addition to maintaining a direct relationship to land and heritage, her horseback riding memoirs resulted in two published books about the wilderness ranch. She had ridden her horse right into the winds of grief, and stayed with her journey until she emerged on the other side of the pain, alive, well, and still connected in an intimate yet different way to her beloved wilderness home.

After awakening that evening at the Santa Anita slough "mussel bake," which was also shortly after my father's death in 1980, I began to visit my aunt and uncle occasionally when they were on their portion of the ranch. Not only was this the beginning of my reconnection to the ranch, it was the beginning of a deep intimacy with my aunt and uncle. I felt blessed to be able to once again connect with my childhood stomping grounds.

Beyond the wonderful growing relationship with Aunt Jane and Uncle Jo, what I noticed most was the silence. When I was growing up immersed in silence, I never noticed it at all. But now the silence was very apparent. During my fifteen-year hiatus from the ranch, I had lived in various urban places. My mind had grown accustomed to noise: car engines running, horns honking, tires on roads nearby as well as the distant drone of tires on highways, my own voice and the voices of others, televisions and radios, the cacophony of crowded places, rock concerts and sporting events, screams of jubilation—noise on and on, relentless, ubiquitous, ever-increasing noise. And beyond those external noises, I had grown accustomed to the incessant chatter of my own mind, which, quite dysfunctionally, resonated with all the external noise, all culminating together in an ever-fluctuating yet constant anxiety, whispering to me day and night.

Entrenched in the modern-day mania that flew over the top of my agitated inner life, I would jump behind the wheel of my suburban Jeep and speed out to the ranch to visit Jane and Jo. As soon as I arrived I would turn off the engine, and there it was, all around me: pure silence screaming at me. There is nothing more alarmingly loud to a mind filled with urban racket than the no-sound sound of the silence of wilderness. It is a deafening attack on the inner–outer ado, piercing the city-saturated psyche to the center. Once the car door opened and the engine was off, there I was, once again, standing alone in the silence.

My intense awareness of the silence at the ranch led me to remember the silence I had experienced while growing up, although I really had not noticed it at the time. But in fact, on the ranch silence was a life-style. Of course, inside the houses where the family lived there was some noise, in the form of conversation. But even the conversation was minimal, as ranch and farm families simply do not talk much. I remember a story my aunt told me about a morning she had spent with her father, my grandfather, when she was quite young. She had timidly asked to accompany him in the ranch Jeep as he went about his daily work. He agreed, so long as there was no conversation! My aunt was perfectly fine with that, as she really just wanted to spend time with her father. Though to many this may seem an unusual and perhaps somewhat cruel request, it is representative of an understanding of the value of silence.

Silence was a central part of living in the wilderness. As a child I didn't consciously think of silence as something of value; it was, rather, taken for granted. Silence was everywhere. Wherever we went on the ranch, there was silence. On early morning hunts, once the conversation in the Jeeps stopped and the sound of the Jeeps had moved off into the distance, leaving me all alone in the backcountry to walk down a canyon, there was the silence. In the morning the silence was most apparent, broken only by the intermittent song of a meadowlark in the distance, the call of quail gathering their coveys together, the distant drone of the foghorn at Point Conception, or the soft surge of a ridgetop breeze brushing the manzanita. Other than sounds like these, sounds that are harmonious with silence, there was absolute still silence all around.

When I was ten, eleven, and twelve, and even younger, my experience of silence and the realization that I was alone in the wild parts of a wild place brought forth an initial fear. What seems to be a primordial preparation for this experience manifests itself in one's digestive system needing to be as light as possible. Perhaps it is the body preparing itself for confrontation with or flight from danger that stimulates the need to be clear and light. It is a mystery, but it was a consistent fact for me as a child. For lack of better preparation at home, the result was an urgent raw and vulnerable confrontation, a brush with the brush, if you will. At such moments, which I kept as brief as possible, my mind and especially my ear became sharply attuned to whatever sounds there were in the surrounding silence, and this, of course, drew my experience into full focus on the silence itself.

Once one is truly inside silence, beyond the vulnerability described above and the initial experience of fear, there is serenity, a peacefulness that begins to enter the body and mind. Then a kind of exhilaration begins to creep in. Whatever fear there was, at least for me, drifted away, and what emerged was a sense of well-being and harmony with the environment. The silence evoked an altered state. It was the doorway to a dreamlike time and space. Once inside this state of being, I felt a resonance with plant and animal life on a much deeper level than normal consciousness. From silence, the understanding that I was not really alone out there in the wild began to emerge.

But, reaching that place of serenity and interconnectedness only occurred after the silence had facilitated a confrontation with myself. Even as a child I felt awkward experiencing myself without any distractions from man-made noise. In silence there is you, and then there is you. Whatever is going on inside yourself becomes very apparent when you are completely surrounded by silence. Whether it is the cognitive chatter in your head and or the deeper emotions within, the way you walk in life is exemplified or mirrored by the way you walk in silence. Whoever or however you are, you are reflected back to yourself by the mirror of silence.

Like everything in life, walking in silence involves a process. I can remember the very beginning of my walks down the canyons after having been left off. At first, whatever thoughts were rumbling in my head became apparent in the silence, and the uselessness of all those thoughts soon become very apparent too. I realized over and over again that if I were to remain inside my thoughts, I would not see what was outside of me. I would not see anything. Realizing how preoccupied I was with my inner self, I became aware how noisy I was as I walked, how hard I was breathing, and how myopic my vision was. Stepping on twigs, breathing loudly and irregularly, staring straight ahead at the trail, shoving my way though brush, all became noticeable against the background of silence. My personal awkwardness, my lack of relationship to my environment, and my utter self-absorption all became clear to me very quickly when I was alone in silence.

In order to respect the silence by attempting to walk silently, I needed to slow way down. My breath needed to be longer, deeper, and more balanced, altogether quieter. I had to pay attention to where I was walking, and avoid aggressive crashing through the bushes. I needed to be aware of and relate to my environment intimately, to move with it rather than against it, quieter, slower, always. Like in darkness, I needed to change my way of seeing, moving from microscopic to macroscopic vision so as to see as much as possible, for simple observation as well as to avoid danger. If I failed in any of those, the silence would bring this quickly to my awareness.

Consequently, walking silently in silence brought about a heightened awareness of the world within me and called upon me to relate to the world about me in a very specific way. It was a world of relationship, a world of interconnection and inter-change, a world of reciprocity. The more intimate I became with my environment, the more intimate it would become with me. Once I adopted that frame of reference, I could find animals before they found me. All of this began with silence.

However, the fact that this silence was available to all of us who frequented the ranch, did not mean that we all related to it in the same way. Many of my peers, as well as many adults, clearly didn't understand what to do with silence. In fact, I sensed that many were very uncomfortable with it and seemed to need to fill it with movement and talk. They could not be still. It seemed to me that they just didn't get it. As people they seemed unsteady, less solid in some way, less trustworthy. Consequently I kept my distance from them, choosing to be around those who could be quiet and still and let the silence have its say. People who were uncomfortable with silence were not good hunters, either. They simply didn't see much of what they were hunting. They were too busy inside, and way too busy outside.

Silence, then, became a kind of portal for me as a young boy and man growing up on the ranch. On one side of the door, there was myself with my everyday mindfulness. On the other side was a huge world that led me to a much different mind-fulness. And the younger I was, the easier it was to go through that door. There was minimal clutter, for I was much more an insouciant child spirit wandering the wilderness of the ranch. By the time I returned to the ranch after a decade and a half, my more urban-minded psychic prison had acquired some fairly thick walls and stout bars. I struggled to reconnect with the youthful naturalness of being in silence and nature, but at first I just couldn't get there. It took many walks in the purity of the ranch's silence for the layers of civilization built up over fifteen years to slowly peel off.

Now, some thirty years after reconnecting with the ranch, the portal is readily accessible to me, and I can pass through it into that other world almost instantaneously. It only takes shutting off the engine of the car and tuning my ear to the silence, often accompanied by the sound of the wind blowing over the top of manzanita or through oak trees, for me to once again be in that sublime world that nature provides. I am grateful to be reunited with my old companion. I also feel blessed that I had the opportunity to be so intimate with silence and the world it makes available when I was so young and impressionable. Without a relationship to silence and the wilderness world, life would be a far less serene experience.

Rage

A culture that alienates itself from the very ground of
its own being, from wilderness outside (that is to say,
wild nature, the wild, self-contained, self-informing
ecosystems) and from the other wilderness within—
is doomed to a very destructive behavior, ultimately
perhaps self-destructive behavior.

—Gary Snyder, *The Practice of the Wild*

BY THE TIME THE YEAR 1984 BEGAN, my reconnection
with the ranch had deepened over a three-year period. As I
have said, I was sharply aware of the loss I felt, the fifteen years
of depressive denial, the onslaught of sadness I had been confronted with in 1980, and the constant low-grade feeing of being
lost, disinherited, psychologically dismembered. I was alive to the
pain of grief, which was now always with me.

One aspect of grief is anger. When one loses something or
someone of great value, it is natural to feel anger. It can be anger
from simply not wanting to experience pain, or a more intense
anger in which the loss is felt to be profoundly unjust. Almost
any loss can bring about the former kind of anger. The more
extreme kind of anger occurs when an intimate someone or
something is lost abruptly, unexpectedly, and prematurely. When
my uncle and godfather, Jo, died recently at the age of ninety-
four, I felt a deep sadness, but no anger. When one of my best

friends died suddenly at age fifty-one, leaving behind his wife, two teenager children, and a very unfinished life, I felt sadness, anger over his premature death, and some fear of my own mortality. It was a loss that felt poignantly unfair, a cruel blow by death's randomness.

There is, however, another kind of loss that can be even more severe. This is a loss of something or someone where there is some barbaric quality to the loss. This kind of loss brings forth a much more primitive form of anger, which is best captured within the word "rage." Fury, violence, wrath, frenzy, passion, madness—these are the qualities of rage. Rage is the ultimate anger. With this kind of anger, one feels primitively out of control. Rage acts either inside one's self, as in being enraged—implosion—or rage acting outwardly from one's self, as in being outraged—explosion. Or both, which can result in a flooding of anger that is overwhelming.

To momentarily digress from rage, for seventeen years most of my free time was spent in relationship with the wilderness of the ranch. I was raised on the ranch and, in a significant emotional way, I was raised *by* the ranch. I say "by" because the experience I had while growing up on the ranch developed, guided, and shaped me. The ranch wilderness was like a third parent or a mentor. The ranch wilderness was like a deeply beloved family member, and it had been an intrinsic family member for more than four generations. Though my direct involvement with that wilderness spanned only a sixteen-year period prior to the sale, there were three generations and one hundred years of fam-ily that walked with me genetically. My heritage and the ancestors therein were always behind and inside me as I wandered over ridges, through brush, along beaches, day and night.

It was also at that time, 1984 or 1985, that I wrestled directly with my heritage. My father had died in 1980, two weeks after I returned home from many years studying. It became quite clear to me that his death was the result of his gradually waning zest for life, which began when the ranch slipped through his hands back in 1965. As I had come to understand, losing the ranch was the ultimate cause of his heart attack fifteen years later. Having reconnected with the ranch and become immersed in my own emotional relationship to the land, I was better able to sort out who my father was and why he made the choices he did. This re-bonding with my father was facilitated by the growing intimacy between me and my Aunt Jane.

When I escaped from the consciousness of city life to Jane's property, situated at the entrance to the western gate, the entrance to the other world in Chumash mythology, the threshold over which souls pass from physical life into spirit life, I found myself in front of my father's twin. As I stared into her eyes, I was staring into the eyes of my father, my grandfather, and my great-grandfather. The experience was something like putting my finger into a light socket, except that the charge was positively magical and life-generating. It was as if the great mystery of my personal universe, heretofore a fog bank, had suddenly become a clear, sunny day.

It was also at this time that my first child, my son, was born. Becoming a father was probably the root of my confrontation with my family heritage. What could I leave to my son that might connect him to his wilderness heritage? It was imperative to me that he have a relationship to land and an understanding of how land was a significant part of his family history. It was with this in mind that I began to take my son to the ranch when I visited with my aunt.

Back to rage. As I drove out of town to the ranch, I told my son stories about places, people, and adventures I had while growing up on the ranch, and I pointed out and named the birds, plants, and animals, in the same way my father had with me and his father had with him. But at the same time there was something else happening on the ranch that was far less life-generating than what was happening between my son and me.

In 1984, sometime between June 4 and July 9, in a series of long meetings filled with political and technical spinning, Santa Barbara County granted Chevron and Texaco permission to transport oil from three offshore oil platforms via pipelines to a processing plant that would be built just east of Gaviota State Park. The pipelines would come from the Point Arguello field, come ashore just north of Point Conception, and run underground along the coastline of the Bixby Cojo Ranch and through the Hollister Ranch, terminating at the processing plant south of Gaviota. Though initially there was supposed to be only one pipeline, it soon became evident that there would be a second pipeline as well. The second pipeline, twenty inches in diameter, would carry sour gas under extreme pressure. The sour gas contained deadly hydrogen sulfide, H2S, in concentrations of 6,000 to 7,000 parts per million. Chevron claimed it would be safe.

Hydrogen sulfide is a naturally occurring compound, a product of cataclysmic processing far beneath the earth's surface. It is common in vapors from volcanoes and is often associated with the fetid air of mineral springs. "Stink camp" is the dysphemism used to describe the pungent odor of hydrogen sulfide, which is similar to that of rotten eggs. However the odor of rotten eggs is not noticeable with sour gas in high concentrations. Oddly, the human olfactory sense shuts down and humans cannot smell hydrogen sulfide at concentrations above 150 parts per million.

Chevron claimed that 7,000 to 9,000 parts per million was a non-lethal concentration of gas, and that only 6,000 parts per million would be transported. But research by those who opposed the pipeline showed that 6,000 parts per million was, in fact, lethal and that the actual concentration that would be transported was 17,000 parts per million. The point here is that not only would this pipeline cross twenty-eight drainages and nineteen environmentally sensitive habitat areas, impacting coastal streams, lagoons, woodlands, upland habitats, and rare species while crossing steep slopes with unstable soils; but also this gas, if inhaled due to a leak, would kill a person in zero to two minutes. Hence its nickname, "two-step gas." Death would come without any warning at all—as if that mattered. Death is death, warning or none.

But this chapter is not about the politics of Chevron and Santa Barbara County. It is about the emotional relationship to a certain personal wilderness. With the proposed laying of this pipeline of toxic gas through the land so intimately connected to my childhood, the stage was set for me to have some rather intense emotions. The scenario unfolded as follows. I would be in my car with my son, driving up to the ranch. I would be filled with deep happiness and excitement in anticipation of visiting my aunt and uncle as well as sharing some "animal" adventures with my son. We would reach the gatehouse where owners checked through, something that had always been offensive to me. Once past the gate, we would begin to look for hawks, wild pigs, bobcats, rabbits, coyotes, and quail while we recalled the places we had seen animals before.

But now there was something else to behold. Chevron had begun to construct their pipelines. When I came upon their "progress," I was stricken by a flood of intense rage throughout my body. It was a feeling that was hard to contain as it is to put into words. At each visit, the ditch they had dug had grown larger. The huge ditch Chevron had dug inched its way along the lower portion of the ranch, parallel to the ranch road, over hills, through creeks, and slowly on and on toward its ultimate destination, the Gaviota refinery.

Initially, my mind would not advance so far as to imagine what would ultimately be placed in the ditch. I was simply overwhelmed by the rape and scarring of my beloved ranchland. It felt as if I were tied up and forced to watch some demonic entity slowly cutting my mother's skin, slicing her gradually from head to toe. I was outraged, enraged, overwhelmed by rage. I was possessed by fantasies of revenge, completely irrational, but my soul sought some outlet for my feelings of rage.

The scarring went on and on, finally resulting in the laying of the pipeline. At this stage there was another layer added to this emotional experience. Now my son and I were confronted by something that went beyond the cutting. We came to the gate one day and were handed instructions for what to do should there be a leak of two-step gas from the pipeline now lying beneath the skin of my "mother" ranch wilderness. The instructions would of course only be helpful if my son and I were not already dead. They stressed the importance of stopping the car if one heard sirens announcing a leak, closing the windows, and sealing the window cracks with tape, then waiting for clearance. The juxtaposition of the life-force I experienced in my reconnection with the ranch while my son was with me, alongside the realization that beneath the surface of my wilderness heritage was a poisonous gas that could instantly kill me and, even more importantly, my son, was an emotional mix I will probably never experience again: Eros and Thanatos, polar opposites united in a single response of rage, violent anger, wrath, frenzy, passion, and madness.

This rage was the most intense of all the emotions I experienced in my grief for the loss of the ranch. The sadness, anger, and disorientation had been minor in comparison to this rage. The scarring of this pristine wilderness by the powers of progress felt like a personal assault. Admittedly, I was in a raw state already. But that is not the point. The point is that I had an intense relationship with this land. The land had raised me in important ways, and as such, it had a high value to me, love.

There was a primal, intimate attachment between me and this land, a deeply felt intimacy. The pipeline was a vicious maiming of my loved one.

The pipeline is still there, but it is no longer in use. It ended up being a colossal failure, in that the Point Arguello field never produced what the oil companies thought it would. It still lies beneath the surface of this coastal wilderness, though poisonous gas does not run through it. The brush and grass have grown back so that many people, not so keen of eye, would not notice anything amiss. As for myself, the scar is still visible to my eye and remembered in my heart, and the rage can easily be revisited simply by consciously choosing to see the distinct change in the texture of the grass or chaparral on a hillside. Nature will eventually heal this scar and make it invisible; but that will never completely heal the wound inside me, a wound that will always be lodged in the fact that such an assault happened at all. I will never be able to forget that my beloved family intimate was brutally invaded under the auspices of "progress." And, as we all know, in the relentless pursuit of progress, these scars are occurring every day throughout the world. Rage.

Reuniting with Home

Whatever you can do, or dream you can do, begin it.
Boldness has genius, power, and magic in it.

—W.H. Murray (after Goethe),
The Scottish Himalayan Expedition

IT WAS NOT TOO LONG AFTER the Wyoming quest that
the whole world abruptly and magically changed. After I had
traveled the interior landscapes of repressed grief, anxiety, and
depression, then the reconnection and reawakening, which
launched me into deep sadness, anger, rage, and a general emotional unease, in January of 1999, life changed. I had recently
been looking at properties in the general area of the California
Central Coast, as it was the kind of landscape that had the most
resonance with my childhood terrain. The rolling golden coastal
and inland hills, enhanced by occasional groves of California
oak, had proved to be irreplaceable by other less familiar wildernesses. I was still visiting my aunt and uncle frequently on their
Hollister ranch property, which was still the most soul-soothing
experience in my life to that point. It always seemed to assuage
the ache deep inside of me, at least temporarily.

Then, while I was returning by bus from the L.A. airport after
ten days coaching a youth soccer team in Guadalajara, I got a
call from my wife telling me that Aunt Jane had become very ill
and was in the hospital, close to death. I went directly from the

bus to the hospital, fearful that this was the end of the generation before me. But, quite miraculously, mostly due to my aunt's
resilience, she began to recover. She stubbornly refused to let
her flame go out. She was not done.

However, the family had all gathered, and it was clear to all
that for Jane and her husband, Jo, to keep living on that remote
property at age ninety-four was simply not possible. Thus the
question of what would happen to their ranch property arose.

The decision was very spontaneous. We were gathered at a
hotel near the hospital. There were many decisions to be made,
and when the discussion turned to the future of the property, the
idea of selling it came up immediately, for it seemed that none of
the nuclear family members wanted to take it over. Once again,
I was confronted with the potential sale of the ranch, only now
I was not sixteen years old, I was fifty. I objected to selling the
parcel, and the focus gradually shifted to me. No one else could
or would take over the responsibility for this land. When I realized that it might be possible for me to continue the heritage
of this property now and into future generations, it was simply
an imperative. Whatever it took, I had to make it happen; we all
had to make it happen. There would not be another sale of the
ranch to someone other than family.

At the risk of over-explaining, I have to say that the sym-
bolism of this moment was undeniable. Although acreage in
question had diminished from the 15,000-acre ranch sold in
1965 to the 100 acres now in question, the issue was the same for
the family: Would the land stay in the family, or not? At age sixteen I could not and did not make a difference. But now I could
make a difference. I was determined not to let the same mistake
be made again. I would find a way to reunite myself with the land
and allow my children to have a connection to their heritage. As
a man to the boy in me, and as a father to my children, I had to
acquire this property.

Everyone worked together to make what clearly needed to happen actually happen. This 100-acre parcel, located on the remote northwest ridge in the wildest backcountry part of the old Hollister Ranch, would stay in the family. I would own three-quarters of it, and other family members would own a quarter. The family heritage, even if in diminished form, would continue. Everyone was satisfied with the outcome, none more than I. I felt as though I were Ulysses finally come home, and the experience of being truly home was well beyond gratifying. The circle was complete.

Home is a simple word used very often in our culture. My children use it all the time. "Dad, can you pick me up? I want to come home." They want to come back to the place where they live, their shelter, their house—their own rooms specifically, given that they are teenagers. But when they shut the doors of their rooms, something else happens on a deeper, more personal level. When the doors shut, their rooms become their refuge. They become sacred spaces where they can be with the selves that lie within them. Their rooms are external homes where they can get back to their internal homes. Their homes are their sanctuaries, where they get away from the chaotic distractions of the outside world and get back to themselves, more focused, more centered, more grounded, more personally identified. This is a crucial phenomenon directly related to their personal evolution as human beings. Without this quiet time in their sanctuaries, their homes, they would end up overwhelmed and lost to themselves.

Home is also referred to as "one's native place or country." Though this definition is much broader than my teenage son's and daughter's "home," one is but a metaphor for the other, and the experience of both can be very similar in terms of personal value. The ranch is my native place; it is my home, and when I am there I experience psychological and spiritual definition. I am identified; I am I, so to speak. Words are insufficient to express the completeness I feel when I gaze at the setting sun reflecting off sandstone rocks, hear the rustle of wind-blown oak leaves at dusk, or carve my way through manzanita or sagebrush. Through experiences such as these I know that I will be able to hand down to my children the same land that I experienced as a child, the same land that three generations before me experienced. This brings the word "home" to a profound level. This is truly my native place.

My deep understanding of the psychological and spiritual importance of home was based on confronting the pain of the experience of losing my ranch home. The cliché that one doesn't know what one has until it's gone certainly holds true for me. By acknowledging and grieving for the loss of my wilderness home, I came to understand its true value. Furthermore, reconnecting with and eventually reowning even a portion of my wilderness home underscored the value of this particular wilderness to me. It is, however, my personal speculation that the depth and breadth of my experience was because of the loss of the property and the pain that resulted. Without this loss and the processing of the grief over the loss, I am not sure I would have fully understood what I had. Within the loss, there was much to be understood and learned; and though this narrative is autobiographical and has personal learning in it, there is also learning in it that extends far beyond myself.

Midnight Visit:
Quail Dream

*Something sacred reveals itself within the mundane,
and you know the land knows you are there.*

—Barry Lopez, *Arctic Dreams*

MY STORY OF COMING HOME would not be complete without mentioning one most interesting anecdote, one that was essential for me to experience. What began with a dream, ends in a dream! I had come home to my native place, that which I was identified with and referred to as my home in every sense of the word. But the house that came with the property was not a house I had lived in as a child. In fact, the property itself was, as stated previously, located on the northwestern corner of the old ranch, the wildest part of the ranch as it was originally, "where the bears are." Amazingly, my aunt and uncle, Jane and Jo Wheelwright, had managed to build a house on that remote part of the ranch. This house became their home after their retirement. The house is much like a cave dwelling. It is nestled amid sandstone rock, oak trees, and manzanita and has as its center a thick and impressively wide rectangular glass window, which faces one side of the Cojo Canyon ridge, then the islands of San Miguel and Santa Rosa in the ocean vista beyond—a simply spectacular panorama.

This was where two very unique people lived for almost twenty years before they were forced for health and safety reason to move to Santa Barbara. It was the house where I and many others sat with Jo and Jane in their sacred space and experienced them via endless and rambling dialogues. Both Jungian analysts, Jo would reel off story after story while Jane sat quietly most of the time, but then suddenly she would offer a statement with laser-like perceptivity. They were a classic juxtaposition of extroverted and introverted personalities. Their house was a symbolic representation of their lives. It was filled with artifacts accumulated during long lives filled with psychological and spiritual depth. Much like Jo and Jane, it was filled with spirit and soul.

This was the house that became my house when I took over the property. Certainly I felt some belonging to the house, given my origin and because I was Jo and Jane's nephew, as well as Jane being my father's fraternal twin sister. But this house was so much *their* home. At my core, I felt as if I were trespassing in some way on their physical and spiritual territory.

Jo and Jane had totems, and these totems were beautifully painted on the headboards of their respective beds. Jo had road-runners on his headboard, as both Jo and the roadrunner have very long legs. Jane had a covey of quail. Intuitively, I think Jane's selection of the totem quail symbolically referred to a woman who could fly in her thoughts, but whose thoughts were never far off the ground and always returned to the ground quickly. She would move from one point to the next quickly, but stayed close to the ground always, as the ground was where she was most comfortable in all aspects of her life.

When Jo and Jane moved into town, their headboards with the roadrunners and quail moved with them. I replaced their beds with one of my own. The dream occurred the first night I slept in the house by myself. I had had a couple of nights with my family in the house, during which sleep was restless as I simply could not be relieved of the experience of trespassing. On my first night alone, I fell asleep restlessly again, and I had the following dream.

I was sitting on a large log on the side of a fairly steep hill. The terrain was much like the terrain of Big Sur, California. It was a rather steep hill, and I was seated about halfway down its slope. There was a cottage-like structure above me, the ocean in the distance below me, and chaparral all around me. Just behind me was a small bushy tree, and I began to hear the quiet yet distinct *peck, peck, peck* of quail coming from behind the tree, just over my left shoulder. I looked around and saw a covey of quail moving slowly through the brush on their way down the hill. Though they were a ways away from me, one quail, a female, distinct in her lack of a topknot, separated from the covey and began to come in my direction. She approached me slowly but directly, while the others passed me some distance away on my right. The female eventually hopped onto the log where I was seated, jumped onto my left shoulder, and nestled against the nape of my neck, resting on my shoulder. There was a feeling of deep intimacy with this quail as she remained in this position for some time. Within that prolonged moment, I had a sense of communication between us. The exchange translated into a feeling that everything was just fine, and that there was no need to worry about anything. There was an implicit soft request for me to relax. Then suddenly the moment of communication was over, as the quail jumped back to the log, paused for a second looking up at me, then continued on down the hill, catching up with the rest of her covey. I continued to sit on the log, but now I had a strong feeling of inner peace, a kind of final peace. I had a clear sense that I had been visited by Jane, and that she had given me permission to go ahead and live in her house. I was to make her home my home.

When I awoke from the dream, I distinctly felt that something unresolved had been resolved. I felt as if Jane had given me her blessing. It seemed that a transfer of ownership had taken place, and it had been done in a way that felt absolutely undeniable, so very appropriate in its way of communication, a visit by a quail in dreamtime. When I went to Santa Barbara the next day, I went to visit Jane in her small cottage dwelling, as I wanted to tell her about the dream. When I had finished telling it, she looked at me, eye to eye, and in her inimitable way said to me, "Oh, I like that dream, that's a good one." Nothing more needed to be said by either of us.

Epilogue:
Everyone's Wilderness, External and Internal

...And I have felt
A presence that disturbs me with the joy
Of elevated thoughts; a sense sublime
Of something far more deeply interfused,
Whose dwelling is the light of setting suns,
And the round ocean and the living air,
And the blue sky, and in the mind of man;
A motion and a spirit, that impels
All thinking things, all objects of all thought,
And rolls through all things.

—William Wordsworth, "Lines Composed
a few Miles above Tintern Abbey"

SO THERE IT IS. With the visit by the quail in dreamtime, the circle was complete; a fifty-year journey of childhood immersion, radical disconnection, and gradual reconnection with the land I call home, full circle. Since then my relationship with the land has continued to deepen over the last fifteen years, and I now live full-time in this special wilderness. As I look back on it all from my elderly state in life, the most significant experiences I had growing up on the ranch, as well as the experiences that have meaning for me in my current life here, are aptly represented by William Wordsworth's nine lines above. The

experience he captures is at the core of the experiences that I
have tried to recount here. The beauty that one encounters in
nature, wild nature, brings forth transcendent or altered states
of being. Personally, I experience both "elevated thoughts" as
well as "something far more deeply infused," an ascendant and
descendent quality of joy, personal well-being, and a connection
to something greater than myself in these many encounters with
nature. When I see a pair of red-tailed hawks circling together
high above a green hillside, or a golden eagle soaring in the
clouds, there is a spirit inside of me that flies into the sky with
them—it is uplifting, an ascension, a sense of my spirit flying as
well. When I am down in the canyons, and I see a regal antlered
stag, a wild boar, or oak trees rustling in a powerful wind, a spirit
in me descends. My feet seem to sink into the earth, and I feel
a grounded essence, a joy deep in my abdomen, an encounter
with duende, soul, and who I am at my core. When I watch the
sun setting over Point Conception on a crystal clear day, or watch
the inland fog roll phantom-like over the northwest corner of
Cojo Ridge, with the full moon as a backdrop, I ascend and
descend. What unites all of these experiences and stimulates
this reverential feeling of something greater than myself yet still
very connected to me is the pristine beauty of the wilderness.
This beauty facilitates upward and downward transcendence,
spirit and soul.

The memories that I have recounted here are all memories of ranch wilderness beauty. My reaction to the blue-winged
teal that flew into the Santa Anita slough and ignited my deep
sense of loss, grief, and need to reconnect with the ranch was
a response to the beauty of countless images experienced in
my youth that were deeply embedded in my memory. The
black brant, the Pacifico deer, the exquisite greens of spring,
sea spray from an offshore breeze, the wind through the oak
trees, the chaparral and eucalyptus, hunting magic, the storm,

the rhythm of horse, cow, and canyon—are all recollections of nature's beauty and still remain alive inside of me because they are experiences of "a sense sublime / Of something far more deeply interfused." When I was growing up and experiencing these images and moments, there were no words like "ascend" and "descend," as there are now, only the pristine experience of this beauty and its unfettered resonance with instinct.

There is nothing new in this, however. For many people the beauty in nature has always been an experience of transcendence, inspirational and reverential. What has motivated the telling of this personal story is the experience of having been so intimately involved with nature's beauty at such an impressionable age, then losing it all completely; then, blessedly, reconnecting with the beauty that was lost, remerging.

At the center of this story is the loss, and the deep feeling and understanding of what was lost, the grief over losing land that was intimate to my life, which came to me in such an explosive and surprising burst of understanding. Wilderness is being lost every second of the day. People who have had a relationship with nature's beauty are excruciatingly aware of this. The battle between environmentalists and developers rages on relentlessly, and will continue to do so. My words could be regarded as environmental advocacy, but ultimately these words are not political, they are experiential. They are gathered in an attempt to render a more personal account of what is being lost, psychologically and spiritually, as we lose our wilderness piece by piece. What is being lost in the physical elimination of wilderness? What is being lost in our growing cultural detachment from the experience of wilderness?

So, at the risk of some redundancy, let me close with this. The words "ascent" and "descent" are chosen very deliberately. Both refer to a transcendent experience, one that goes beyond ordinary limits or common experience, something surpassing the usual, especially the urban usual. Respectively, transcendent ascent and descent via nature provide us humans with different information about ourselves. Within ascent there is creativity and imagination. Ideas are generated in this flight of spirit, and they can result in a brush with ecstasy. An exhilaration and excitement can be experienced in this creative flight; problems can be solved, paradigms can shift, original ideas can be generated. This is a highly fertile mental, emotional, and spiritual experience, and has something to do with our personal connection to everything on the planet.

The descendant response to nature's beauty takes us downward to another imperative place of being. Here the world of instinct is experienced and can be harnessed as a guide. The ground-level perspective cuts through all the manic hoopla of the civilized world and offers a reality that is crystal clear in the truth it makes available. Problems that were problems, confusion that was confusion, melt away as the world of instinct cuts a clear path through the chaos. Without access to the realm of instinct, the world and the human condition, especially in its relationship to the modern world, can become intensely complicated. It can be very easy to be lost to one's self without a direct connection to the instinctual life that nature can give us. With a connection to instinct, we are more able to see who we really are in our unique persona selves—our personal souls, if you will—that which is truly ours. And nature is the guide to this realm.

So, on this early morning as I sit at my desk, it is all happening again as I look through the window far out to the west. The early morning ridge fog is drifting over the manzanita, thick and phantom-like. The sound of the wind and the knocking of the sliding wooden door reach my ear, and I experience a soulful or soul-filled sinking and deepening response to what is around me, descent, and the grounded world of instinct is at hand. The fog then lifts slightly, and through the glass, over the rolling spring-green hills, I see the sunlit glimmer of the Point Conception lighthouse in the distance, just beyond the gray-white airy density surrounding me. I experience a soaring spirit inside as I see the beauty of sunlight magnifying the wonder of the California coastline where it abruptly changes its course. The generative spirit of ascent is at hand, and the words begin to flow, guided by my connection to instinct. It is all happening right now, that "sense sublime" is present, nature's beauty is everywhere, and the question necessarily still sits with me, as it always does and probably always will, in an ongoing, haunting way: "What is being lost when we lose our intimacy with nature and wilderness?"

It is time to go outside for a walk. I will, undoubtedly, continue to consider this question. As for now, enough said.

> *In beauty, I walk*
> *Beauty before me*
> *Beauty behind me*
> *Beauty above me*
> *Beauty below me*
> *Beauty within me*
> *In beauty, I walk.*
>
> —Navajo chant

CPSIA information can be obtained
at www.ICGtesting.com
Printed in the USA
LVHW101816211222
735705LV00003B/432